MALTA
and its islands:
GOZO AND COMINO

Miller Distributors Limited
Miller House, Airport Way, Tarxi
P.O. Box 25, Malta International A
Telephone: (356) 21 66 44 88 Facs
Web address: www.millermalta.com

BONECHI

plurigraf

Editorial management: Monica Bonechi
Graphic design, picture research
and cover: Sonia Gottardo
Layout: Sonia Gottardo
Maps: Stefano Benini

The photographs belong to the archive of
Casa Editrice Bonechi
and were taken by Andrea Fantauzzo.
Other sources: Archivio Plurigraf, Kevin Casha,
Daniel Borg, Jonathan Beacom & Perfecta Advertising.
Photo p. 17: Christine Muscat Azzopardi (courtesy
of Miller Distributors Limited).
Photos pp. 95 above, 96/97: Marka (© Walter Bibikow).
The photos of the Gozo Cathedral (p. 113, 114 above left)
were taken and printed by the courtesy of the
Cathedral Chapter.

The publisher will be grateful for information concerning
the sources of photographs without credits and will be
pleased to acknowledge them in future editions.

A 10 9 8 7 6 5 4 3 2

Introduction

The Republic of Malta is located in the centre of the Mediterranean Sea. The archipelago is formed of two main islands, Malta and Gozo which, as well as Comino, are the only inhabited islands, and some smaller uninhabited islands named Cominotto, Filfla and St Paul. Thanks to its position, Malta has represented a bridge between Europe and Africa since ancient times. The islands are in fact only 90 kilometres from Sicily and 290 from the African coast. With a population of about 400,000 inhabitants and a surface area of 320 km^2, Malta has the highest density of population per square kilometre of any European country.

Numerous peoples have occupied these islands in the course of its lengthy history (Phoenicians, Romans, Arabs, Normans, Spanish, French and English) leaving behind an artistic and cultural heritage of immense value. As early as prehistoric times large temples were built indicating a highly developed and sophisticated civilization. It was, however, under the Order of the Knights of Saint John that Malta developed culturally and artistically and the island was enhanced with beautiful palaces, churches, fortifications and works of art. With its mild climate, clear sea, impressive cliffs and the bright colours of the Mediterranean shrubs, this group of islands is a true paradise and an ideal destination for holidays of all kinds.

The Maltese have traces of all the various peoples who have lived in Malta and combine the traits of many ethnic groups, although characteristic Semitic and Anglo-Saxon features are predominant. Most of the population is, however, of Arab descent. The Catholic religion is practised by 90 per cent of the inhabitants.

The official languages are Maltese and English. The former is of Semitic origin and the vocabulary contains a wealth of words with neo-Latin and Anglo-Saxon origins. There are numerous instances of the Arab influence, which lasted some 300 years, especially in the grammatical structure of the language, as well as in the vocabulary. Italian was the official language of the Knights of the Order of St John and until 1934 also of culture and the ruling classes and is therefore still quite common today.

Prehistory

St Paul

The earliest Maltese settlements date from the Stone Age: it was during this period that the first inhabitants arrived from Sicily bringing with them seeds, domestic animals and oxydian utensils. These peoples were farmers but they also built numerous temples making use of enormous blocks of stone as can still be seen at the Tarxien site. About 1800 BC, however, this population disappeared for reasons that are still unknown. Subsequently Malta was occupied by peoples who lived from pasture farming and worked bronze but were much less civilised than their predecessors. During the Iron Age more new arrivals established themselves on the island as can be seen at the settlement of Baħrija (900 BC); these new colonisers lived in harmony with the existing inhabitants and became entirely integrated.

The Phoenicians arrived in Malta about 800 BC. They immediately understood the strategic importance of the archipelago and established several colonies, thus influencing the way life, culture and language of the inhabitants. The name "Malta" is derived from *Mlt* (shelter, anchorage) the name used by the Phoenicians to describe the island. With the fall of Phoenicia, Carthage took possession of the island; after the Punic wars and the defeat of Carthage, it became part of the Roman Empire. During this period Malta experienced an important phase of development – irrigation systems were constructed and methods of cultivating on a large scale were introduced. Linen, honey, wax and olive oil were all produced and exported. The Romans also built new cities: Melita in the area that is now Mdina and Rabat, and Gaulos on Gozo (now Victoria).

St Paul was shipwrecked on Malta in 60 AD, as is recounted in the Acts of the Apostles, and during the three months that he remained on the island he succeeded in establishing a strong base for the development of Christianity. Under arrest, the saint was being transported to Rome in order to stand judgement in front of Caesar. However, the ship on which he was travelling lost its bearings during a storm and after 14 days it arrived at what is now Qawra Point. St Paul lived in a cave (now St Paul's Grotto at Rabat) but he was allowed considerable freedom of movement and succeeded in converting both Malta and Gozo. Catacombs were later built near to the cave but were never used as a refuge mainly because there is no evidence of any persecution in the archipelago. In 250 AD St Agatha also found refuge on Malta as she fled from persecution in Catania.

Byzantine Domination

The Arabs

The Middle Ages

When the Roman Empire split into two parts, the islands of Malta were included in the eastern empire which had its capital in Byzantium. Little is known of the history of Malta in the four centuries following 400 AD. Around 650 AD the possessions of the Eastern Roman Empire were organised into military provinces. Towards the end of the 7th century sources record the name of Arconte of Malta who, faced with the threat of invasion by the Muslims, seized military and civil command. Malta was most probably a powerful naval base for the Byzantine fleet in this period, however the living conditions for the inhabitants were extremely poor. Most of the population would appear to have lived in a semi barbarous state as the few remains dating from the Byzantine period seem to indicate.

In 870 the Arabs conquered Malta. Christian forces struggled determinedly to defend the islands but were finally subdued by the invaders. The Arabs did not however, treat the Maltese harshly and despite imposing Islam as the state religion they did, however, tolerate the Christian beliefs of the inhabitants. The Arabs introduced new crops (cotton and citrus fruits) and new irrigation systems. They also extended and built new fortifications. And to better protect the territory they had conquered they created a ditch to isolate part of the city of Melita, thus creating Mdina. The strongest traces left by Arab domination are to be found in the Maltese language, however.

Arab domination ended with the arrival of the Normans lead by Count Roger in 1090. Legend relates that the Maltese flag was created by Roger when he tore off part of his own red and white flag and gave it to the people of Malta. The Maltese aristocracy came into being during the Norman period leading to the building of many palaces which enhanced the cities of the archipelago, especially Mdina. At the same time Christianity became firmly established and numerous religious orders took up residence in the islands. Following Norman domination Malta was ruled by various aristocracies, including the German and French. Throughout the Middle Ages the islands were constantly attacked by pirates who kidnapped and enslaved the inhabitants.

The Knights of the Order of St John

The Great Siege

The Foundation of Valletta

In 1530 Emperor Charles V gave the Maltese islands to the Knights of St John and the 250 years of their rule are the most illustrious in the history of the archipelago. The population welcomed the Order in the hope that they would enjoy greater protection from assault by the pirates. Attacked by the Turks in 1547 and 1551, the Knights were obliged to build numerous fortifications such as Fort St Angelo and Fort St Elmo on the north coast of Malta.

The Order built new churches and palaces as well as aqueducts, and art too underwent a revival. Commerce and trade also intensified during this period. Doubtless one of the most important heritages left to Malta by the Knights is the eight pointed cross, now indeed known as the 'Maltese Cross'.

In 1565 the Turks attempted to invade Malta with the intention of taking the entire archipelago and using it as a base to penetrate Europe. The Ottoman army consisted of some 48,000 men while the Maltese had only 8,000. The Grand Master, La Valette, head of the Order of the Knights, decided not to deploy his men on the beaches to face the attack, but instead organised his defence from within the fortifications. Fort St Elmo failed to resist siege by the Turks and was forced to capitulate, allowing the Ottomans to then turn their attention to Vittoriosa and Senglea. With the arrival of reinforcements from Sicily the Maltese were able to repulse the Turks who were finally forced to withdraw. By safeguarding Malta, Europe too was saved from attack by the Turks and in recognition of this the rulers of Europe sent help to the country thus contributing to the building of a new city.

Named after the Grand Master de la Valette, the foundation stone of Valletta was laid on 28 March 1566. Pope Pius IV sent his military engineer, Francesco Laparelli, who planned the city according to two principles: it was to be both a stronghold of Christianity and an architectural masterpiece. Valletta was designed with a grid pattern and was equipped with running water and a drainage system. When Laparelli left the island work was continued by his Maltese assistant, Gerolamo Cassar, who was responsible for the most important buildings belonging to the Order. La Valette died in 1568 and the Grand Masters who succeeded him continued to embellish the city with further palaces. The houses of artisans and employees of the Order were located in less important streets.

The decline of the Order

The French The British

The Way to Independence

With the establishment of their headquarters on Malta, the Knights of St John became the first governors of the Maltese to actually live on the island, thus facilitating growth and development in the archipelago. A programme of public works was initiated and many of the Maltese found work with the Order. The most gifted citizens were encouraged to study abroad and foreign artists were invited to the island and have left behind a great artistic heritage; in 1769 moreover, the university was founded. Yet in the 18th century the Order began to fall into decline creating unemployment and, with the finances of the Knights now in a precarious state, poverty set in. The last Grand Master, Ferdinand von Hompesch was elected just as Napoleon was preparing to invade the archipelago.

Napoleon took possession of Malta in 1798. The Emperor of France abolished slavery and freed the small group of slaves living on the island as well as closing the university and abolishing the aristocracy. Despite this, the people of Malta were not content under French dominion and decided to rebel. They first sought help from the king of Sicily (the Knights ruled Malta as a domain of the Kingdom of the Two Sicilies) and later from the British. When the French were driven out it was decided that Malta should again be governed by an Order of the Knights although the Maltese protested. The archipelago became part of the British Empire in 1814 and, until its final independence, Malta experienced a new period of splendour mainly because its position in the heart of the Mediterranean was very strategic and well exploited by the British.

In 1921 the British conceded a form of self-government and a constitution to Malta. During the First World War the island was known as the "Nurse of the Mediterranean" as it was an important refuelling station and base for hospitalising the wounded. During the Second World War, King George VI conferred the Cross of St George on the Maltese people for the courage they had demonstrated. Following the war the call for independence from the British Empire increased however and a degree of autonomy within the Commonwealth was obtained in 1964 while the republic was established in 1974. It was not until 1979, however, that the English left Malta completely; on 1 May 2004 the Republic of Malta became part of the European Union.

Valletta

When Grand Master Jean Parisot de la Valette laid the foundation stone of Humilissima Civitas Vallettae, the last thing that he had in mind was a city of fine palaces. Valletta was intended as a fortress to protect the two harbours on either side of the rocky peninsula on which it was to be built. According to tradition, the Church of Our Lady of Victories was built over the foundation stone itself. The façade of the church was altered in 1690 but is otherwise unchanged.

The first buildings to be erected were the Auberges: these were the headquarters of the different nationalities to which the Knights belonged. Other buildings followed and quite rapidly the entire area was occupied by imposing palaces and churches. Space is still at a premium in Valletta and no building is wasted: one of the Auberges is the Office of the Prime Minister, one a museum, another the General Post Office and two are Government Departments. One was demolished in 1839 to make way for the Anglican Cathedral of St Paul. Palazzo Lanfreducci was also demolished and in its place the Royal Opera House was built; finished in 1866 it was destroyed by enemy bombing in 1942. A block away from the ruins of the Royal Opera House is Strait Street, which was better known among sailors of the British Navy as "The Gut". Here soldiers and sailors spent their evenings in activities far removed

The **National Library**, the Biblioteca, was the last building to have been commissioned by the Order and was finished in 1796. It houses a rich collection of books as well as medieval manuscripts and the archives of the Order. For those interested in things military there is the **Palace Armoury**, the **War Museum** in Fort St Elmo and an exact replica of the underground War Room in the Lascaris Ditch. Even if the Opera House has yet to rise from the ashes of the Blitz (some are of the opinion that a multi-storey car park should be built there instead), music lovers and balletomanes can still go to **Manoel Theatre**. This gem of a building dates from 1732 and has recently been restored to its former glory for, as its builder Grand Master Anton Manoel de Vilhena would have said, "... the honest recreation of the people". For art lovers there are the **Museum of Fine Arts** and the **Cathedral Museum**. Valletta boasts three parish churches and a host of others, but pride of place must go to **St John's Co-Cathedral**. The sombre exterior of this edifice entirely belies the sumptuous interior: no space is left unadorned, the walls are carved and gilded and the painted vaulted ceiling is a masterpiece by Mattia Preti, while four hundred slabs of inlaid marble pave the church. These slabs are emblazoned with the armorial bearings of the most important members of the Order. Even a walk around the streets of Valletta can be rewarding, as long as one does not walk too fast. Many admire the magnificent Baroque façade of the Castellana, the Law Courts of the Order, few, however, notice a large iron hook let into the wall just around the corner of this building. Nobody can say for certain who put it there or why (one theory is that it was used in hoisting the bells of St. John's Co-Cathedral across the square) but to the sailors of the British Navy this hook possessed magical powers: they believed that any sailor who passed through it unaided would be promoted.

from Grand Opera as the bars and the ladies in the Gut did a roaring trade; the only indication of its boisterous past are the fading sign-boards outside the establishments on Strait Street.

A number of Government departments were obliged to move out of Valletta due to lack of space. The University was transferred to more modern premises and several other institutions followed suit. Most, if not all, foreign missions have also moved out of Valletta, a notable exception being the Embassy of the Sovereign Military Hospitaller Order of St John of Jerusalem, of Rhodes and of Malta - known as the Knights of Malta. This embassy is housed in St. John's Bastion.

Some of the older parts of Valletta have been pulled down; these relics from previous centuries were quaint and picturesque but were, at the same time, inadequate and unhealthy. The new constructions, however, have been carried out tastefully and, as a rule, do not jar with the older buildings of Valletta.

THE DEFENSIVE WALLS AND ST JAMES' BASTION

The urban centre of Valletta is surrounded and protected by ancient city walls with imposing ramparts that represent not only the main structure of a complex defensive system but also a splendid and perfect example of the most advanced 15th-century military engineering; the arrangement and development of the town road system and layout is still inevitably influenced by these defensive structures and their conservation has lead to the recognition of the capital of Malta as a Cultural Heritage site.

The St James' Bastion extends wedge-like in the direction of nearby Floriana and the two mighty defensive fortifications are actually connected.

Below the rampart is a ditch and in 1640 plans were made to widen and deepen this, transforming it into a navigable canal which would have linked the Grand Harbour to Marsamxett. The plan never became a reality but is evidence of the importance that the Maltese always attributed to the town's system of fortifications.

Behind St James' Bastion are further defensive buildings used in the past as munitions and gunpowder deposits and as safe storage for the artillery. Of particular note are the St James' Cavalier and St John's Cavalier, also known as St John's Bastion where, since 1968, the Embassy of the Sovereign Military Hospitaller Order of St John of Jerusalem, of Rhodes and Malta is housed.

An aerial view clearly showing the impressive defensive structures that encircle Valletta. In the centre, on either side of the City Gate are St James' Bastion (right) and St John's Cavalier (left).

VALLETTA

THE CITY GATE

A visit to Valletta must certainly begin at the City Gate, the real entrance to the city, built in 1964 over a pre-existing gate and destined to provide a grandiose access to the centre of Valletta which is today almost entirely a pedestrian area. Just through the Gate lies *Freedom Square* where *Republic Street* begins, but a wide open space precedes this which, when Floriana was founded, was kept unencumbered in order to provide a clear range for firing the city's defensive artillery. Today this large square is almost constantly full of buses and in the centre stands the **Triton Fountain**, a 20th-century work by the Maltese sculptor, Vincent Apap. In front of the city walls near to the gate there is still a 17-metre deep ditch, though it is now quite dry. This was dug directly into the solid rock by Turkish slaves to link the Grand Harbour and the port of Marsamxett. The bridge that crosses the ditch leading to the City Gate overlooks a second one below, which carried the railway line connecting Valletta and Mdina from 1883 until 1931.

REPUBLIC STREET

The true centre of La Valetta is without any doubt Republic Street, busy and always crowded and also the longest, widest and most typical of the city. A fascinating pedestrian area stretching from the City Gate to Fort St Elmo, the most prestigious shops, the most important offices, and numerous monumental buildings are located on this important street. Thus, beside the *Auberge de Provence* and the *Grand Master's Palace* right at the beginning of Republic Street at the City Gate end,

Shopping in Republic Street can provide interesting and enjoyable entertainment. At a certain point the road widens to become Queen's Square with the figure of Queen Victoria in the centre. Right by this statue of Victoria, which has survived the archipelago's independence unperturbed, is the renowned Cordina café, a veritable institution in Valletta, flanked by an incredible variety of shops providing an amazing range of choice. However, shopping enthusiasts will find that Valletta is full of quite delightful surprises both for the different types of shop and the products sold there. One has only to think of the precious Maltese clocks, square, for the wall, with one hand and delicately decorated with gold leaf, or the fantastic creations of goldsmiths, masters in the art of gold and silver work including items made of delicate filigree such as earrings and bracelets. Walking along Republic Street, following the rises and slopes that are so typical of the roads of Valletta, the real lively and vibrating heart of the city is discovered side by side with its most traditional and popular features.

stand two churches almost facing each other on either side of this bustling urban thoroughfare. On one side is the 18th-century **Church of St Barbara**, built by Romano Carapecchia for the "Langue" of Provence while on the other is the **Church of St Francis** which has experienced various quite important phases in its history such as the complete reconstruction commissioned by the Grand Master Carafa in 1681, and considerable enlargement that took place in 1920. In the central section of Republic Street is the building of the *National Library of Malta*; lastly is the 16th-century **Casa Rocca Piccola**, a fine aristocratic residence that the owners have opened to the public with an exhibition of all the household treasures and rooms furnished in period style.

UPPER AND LOWER BARRACCA GARDENS

When the mighty defensive ramparts of Valletta's city walls finally ceased to have a protective function and effectively took on a more urban role, the improvement and enhancement of their appearance became a matter of urgency. Thus this extensive area, occupied by terraces with structures built up against the walls, was quickly reorganised and the artillery which until then had occupied the area, gave way to tranquil and luxuriant gardens. In one part the Upper Barracca Gardens came into being and were originally the favourite spot of the Italian Knights. There is a magnificent view across the Three Cities and the sea within the Grand Harbour from the gardens which also overlook the 18th-century Old Customs House; amidst stone buildings, neat pathways and Mediterranean vegetation there is also a bust of Winston Churchill, a prestigious work by Vincent Apap. In the other section and also overlooking the Grand Harbour are the Lower Barracca Gardens which, built on what was once the Castile Rampart, have a more pleasant and elegant history and extend towards Senglea and Vittoriosa not far away. A relaxing, verdant and shady place for rest and refreshment, with flourishing palms and flower beds as well as delightful panoramic views, the gardens also have a majestic temple in Doric style built in 1810 in honour of

Sir Alexander Ball. Before becoming the first English governor of the island, Ball had distinguished himself as a cunning strategist and commander having considerably contributed to the rebellion of the Maltese against the French occupants at the end of the 18th century. The **Malta Siege Memorial** commemorates another epic resistance struggle, this time in 1942 against Italian and German troops, and especially their air forces. The monument is to the memory of the victims and records the courage shown by the people of this small island during the Second World War, fortitude for which they were awarded the *George Cross*, one of the highest honours to be conferred by King George VI. The monument was inaugurated in 1992 by Queen Elisabeth II.

Opposite page, views of the Upper Barracca Gardens from where, in addition to the row of cannons known as the Saluting Battery, Fort St Angelo can be seen extending into the sea and protecting Senglea behind (above); centre, the image of the old Castile Rampart where the Lower Barracca Gardens now are (three images in this page). Note in particular the form of the Doric temple dedicated to Sir Alexander Ball at the beginning of the 19th century (below).

MELITENSIUM PIETAS

THE CARNIVAL

One of the most important events in the Maltese year, the Carnival was already recorded in 1535, but has been celebrated with particular enthusiasm since 1565 when, in song and dance, children represented the victory over the Turks.

On the Saturday before Lent there is a parade of grotesque figures through the streets of the city, followed by musicians in historic costume and, to permit the carnival floats to pass through, the main city gate has even been altered. A real treat and festival for tourists as well.

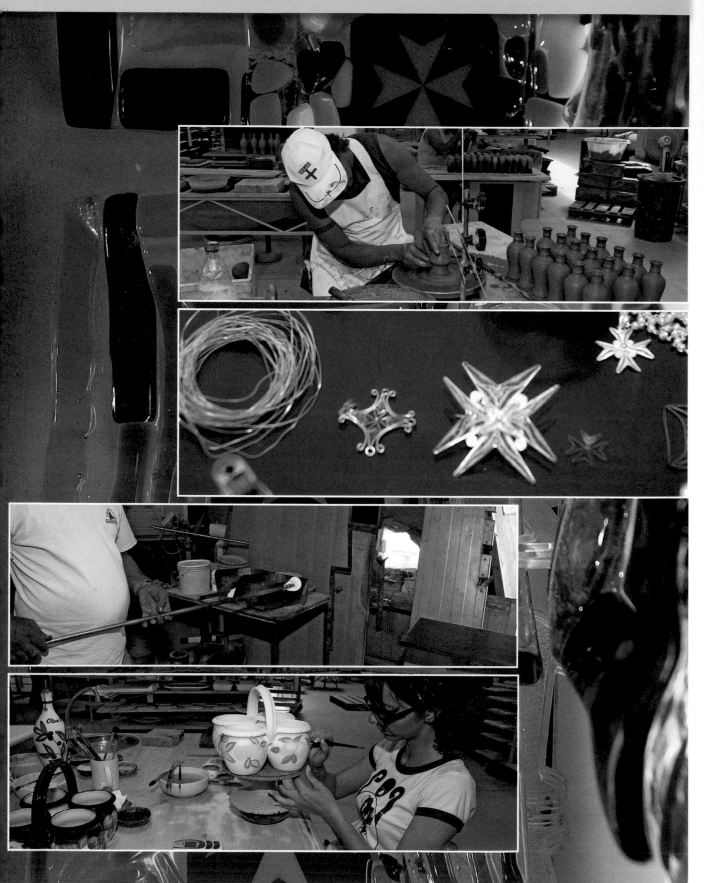

The markets of Malta represent highly popular daily and weekly events for the local population – and for others too. Every town and village has in fact its own market, with its own distinct products and features. Clearly some of the best and most attractive items are the typical fresh products of the archipelago such as the fish. But there is also a full range of goods for the household, clothing, music and toys. Cities such as Valletta have room for more than one market and thus, in addition to the daily one in Merchants Street, there is also the Sunday market of Il-Monti just outside the main entrance to the city, selling interesting antiques. Visiting the markets can therefore also be a fun way of discovering Malta.

MERCHANTS STREET

While Republic Street is the place to go shopping, parallel to it and just as crowded and busy, Merchants Street is clearly the home of the market. Held here every morning it attracts numerous visitors and provides products of all kinds, including an amazing variety of clothing. In the shadow of the traditional wooden balconies there are also many crafts shops where the characteristic filigree is produced as well as terracotta (an ancient tradition), and items of blown glass (an art introduced more recently). There are also famous buildings here, such as the **Auberge d'Italie**, built in the 16th century with one floor only and raised in 1683 by the Grand Master Carafa, and **Palazzo Parisio** where Napoleon stayed in 1798 on his way to Egypt.

Merchants Street, a typical street constantly crowded with tourists and shoppers who visit the picturesque market held here every morning.

The Auberges of the Knights

The Order of the Knights was divided into "Langues" (from 'language' indicating nationality), each of which had an Auberge, as their residence was known, with a chapel, dining hall and other rooms arranged around a courtyard. Originally there were eight Auberges all located in Vittoriosa. When Valletta came into being Auberges were constructed there too – but only seven, as Henry VIII had suppressed the English "Langue" following a dispute with the Pope and consequently the English Knights did not have a residence of their own in the new city. The Auberges were all built by Gerolamo Cassar between 1571 and 1590. Today only five still remain: the Auberge d'Italie in Merchants Street which now also houses the Malta Tourist Authority, the Auberge de Provence in Republic Street, the Auberge d'Aragon, the oldest and simplest structure, the Auberge d'Angleterre et Bavière and the Auberge de Castille.

AUBERGE DE CASTILLE

The Auberge de Castille, Leon and Portugal, is the largest and perhaps finest of all the Auberges and belonged to the Spanish and Portugese "Langues". Its head was the Grand Chancellor of the Order of St John.

It was first built in 1574 by Gerolamo Cassar on a site originally intended for the Magistrates Palace. Extensive reconstruction was undertaken in 1744 during Grand Master Pinto de Fonseca's term of office. Domenico Cachia, the architect responsible for these modifications, was influenced by the Prefecture in Lecce and produced a very imposing façade. Now the prime minister's residence, one of the most impressive features of this building is the large stairway leading from the ground to the first floor, as well as the courtyard, flanked on three sides by an austere portico.

The severe but majestic façade of the Auberge de Castille, which was influenced by the palace of the Prefecture in Lecce.

AUBERGE DE PROVENCE
(ARCHAEOLOGICAL MUSEUM)

The Auberge de Provence was built between 1571 and 1575 to a design by the Maltese architect Gerolamo Cassar. The façade was altered during the first half of the 17th century and its appearance has remained unchanged, with characteristic Doric columns on the ground level, and Ionic pillars on the first floor. The Auberge was the residence of the "Langue" de Provence, its Head, the "Grand Commandeur" being the Treasurer of the Order. From 1820 to 1954 the building housed the British officers' Union Club and following a complete programme of restoration carried out in 1990 it now houses the **National Museum of Archaeology**. This fascinating museum, with its quite unique patrimony of Maltese archaeological items, houses a valuable collection of prehistoric artefacts such as pottery, statuettes (including ten headless statues of fertility goddesses), stone implements, personal and other ornaments recovered from Malta's prehistoric and megalithic temple sites. Several models of these temples are on permanent display and tomb furniture from the Punic and Roman periods is also exhibited. One of the most famous items is the marble stone dating from the 2nd century BC, of a religious nature and engraved with a prayer which, written in both Greek and Phoenician, has enable scholars to decipher the Phoenician alphabet.

Examples of small statues from the megalithic temples of the archipelago, terracotta figures and various utensils exhibited in the Archaeological Museum and, below, a view of one of the rooms showing the attractive display as well as the important and informative photographic documentation.

NATIONAL MUSEUM OF FINE ARTS

South Street is one of the most elegant streets in the city and one of the most graceful palaces located here is *Admiralty House* home to the National Museum of Fine Arts. This was one of the first buildings erected in Valletta, but it was rebuilt in its present form between 1761 and 1765.

During the French occupation it was offered to the Bishop of Malta to be used as a seminary. On the capitulation of the French garrison, "Casa Miasi" as the palace then became known, was occupied by the Commander of the Anglo-Maltese troops, Captain Alexander Ball.

In 1808, Louis Charles, Count of Beaujolais, and his brother Louis Philippe, Duke of Orléans arrived, taking up residence in the palace, and it was here that the Count of Beaujolais died.

The premises were leased to the British naval authorities in 1821 and the palace remained the official residence of the Commander-in-Chief of the British Mediterranean Fleet.

In 1961 it was handed over to the Maltese Government and in 1974 it was restored to its former glory and converted into a Museum of Fine Arts. It houses paintings, sculpture, furniture and objects connected with the Order of St John. The permanent collection includes works by Reni, Valentini, Stormer, Preti, Tiepolo, Favray and Perugino. A section is specially reserved for works by Maltese artists. Temporary exhibitions and lectures are also held here.

Views of the splendid light classical interiors of the Museum of Fine Arts and some of the works of art exhibited there.

ST. JOHN'S CO-CATHEDRAL

In 1573 Grand Master Jean de la Cassière authorized the construction of a conventual church of the Order of St John. It was completed in 1578 by the Maltese architect Gerolamo Cassar.

Its austere exterior gives no indication of the opulent and extravagant interior. A modest portico over the main door supports the balcony used by the Grand Master to present himself to the public after election. Surmounting the façade, Alessandro Algardi's *bas relief* of the Saviour was relocated here in 1850 from its original place in a chapel close to the entrance of the Grand Harbour. The spires on the bell towers were destroyed during the Second World War.

The rectangular baroque **interior** was embellished by successive Grand Masters and further enriched by the "Gioja" or gift, which every Knight was bound by statute to give on admission to the Order.

Between 1662-1667, Mattia Preti "Il Calabrese" painted the *Life of St John the Baptist*, patron saint of the Order, directly on to the primed stone of the ceiling. The Cottoner brothers paid for this work.

The *walls* are covered with carved gilded limestone, and the unique *pavement* contains about 400 sepulchral memorials to the Order's aristocracy. These inlaid marble slabs are adorned with heraldic devices, military and naval trophies, religious motifs, and symbols befitting a necropolis.

Mazzuoli's great marble sculpture of the *Baptism of Christ* dominates the presbytery. The *altar* is made of Lapis lazuli and other rare marbles. The Episcopal throne was originally reserved for the Grand Master.

The side chapels were allotted to each of the "Langues" of the Order and the Grand Masters belonging to each particular langue are buried here.

Zondadari's mausoleum to the left of the main entrance is worth noting as are those of the Cottoner brothers and

The prolific and innovative Maltese architect, Gerolamo Cassar, was born in 1520, probably in Vittoriosa, and died about 1590 in Valletta. Of Sicilian origins, he was summonsed by the Order of the Knights of St John, the new rulers of Malta for whom he had worked on other occasions, to turn the dream of building a new fortified city into a reality. Based on the plans of the Italian engineer, Francesco Laparelli, and with the support and collaboration of Gabrio Serbelloni, work began on the future city of Valletta in 1565. Built on a hill and with a straight main road linking Fort St Elmo to the City Gate, it is no exaggeration to say that the vast majority of buildings were designed or built by Cassar, who is rightly recognised as the builder of Valletta.

Perellos in the Chapel of Aragon. There is also a beautiful *monument* by Pradier *to the Count of Beaujolais*, brother of Louis Philippe of France.

The gates in the **Chapel of the Holy Sacraments**, like the Candlesticks on the main altar, are made of silver. These remaining treasures attest to what was perhaps the wealthiest church in Europe before being plundered by Napoleon in 1798. The Grand Masters who died at Malta before the church was completed are buried in the **Crypt**, the most important sarcophagi being those of La Valette, victor of the Great Siege of 1565 and La Cassière who built St John's.

During the month of June a superb set of *Flemish tapestries*

Caravaggio in Malta

Michelangelo Merisi was born in Milan on 29 September 1571 and was nicknamed Caravaggio after the small town in the province of Bergamo where he spent his childhood. He was already a confirmed artist when he sailed to Malta from Naples in July 1607 to escape from a death sentence for having killed a man in a brawl (1606). Protected by influential friends in Rome, he was put in contact with the then Grand Master of the Knights of St John, Alof de Wignacourt who greatly appreciated Caravaggio's work and therefore commissioned and acquired a portrait. After a period as a novice, on 14 July 1608, Caravaggio was made a Knight of Grace, the rank inferior to the Knights of Justice which was strictly reserved for those of aristocratic birth. Yet even in Malta he was unable to find the tranquillity that, throughout his entire life, seems to have escaped him. He was arrested for a violent argument with a Knight of superior rank and on 6 October 1608 he was imprisoned in St Angelo in Valletta. This event was quickly followed by news of the death sentence that awaited him and to avoid the probable consequences, Caravaggio managed a daring escape from the prison and sailed immediately to Sicily where he took refuge in Syracuse. On 6 December the Knights expelled him from the Order with dishonour, "as a foul and putrid member".

The Beheading of Saint John the Baptist

The only work to have been signed by Caravaggio and by far the largest (oil on canvas, 361 x 520 cm.), the Beheading of St John the Baptist was painted in 1608 for the Oratory of the Co-Cathedral in Valletta and earned the artist the award of the Maltese Cross. But even at a moment when fate seemed to favour him an instinctive and heavy despondency seems to pervade both his painting and himself: the backgrounds are increasingly dark and shadowy and the brushstrokes increasingly rapid. The overall impression is of a dramatic force represented by the device of the Saint's blood which flows into the artist's signature in red, as well as by the figure of John the Baptist lying on the ground and the entire structure of the scene where the dark and austere setting appears to dominate the expressive and tragic participation of the figures.

are hung in the Church. There are fourteen large and an equal number of smaller tapestries copied from paintings by Rubens, Poussin and Preti. The larger ones depict the *Life of Christ* or symbolise the triumph of the Church. The smaller tapestries depict the *Apostles*. During the year these are exhibited in the adjoining **Cathedral Museum** which also contains relics, religious vestments and the treasure of St John's. In the ornate *Oratory* is a 3 by 5 metre painting by Caravaggio depicting the **Beheading of St John**. This painting is regarded as Caravaggio's greatest masterpiece and is the only one of his paintings which bears his signature. The church became a Co-Cathedral with that of Mdina in 1816.

The magnificent interior of the Co-Cathedral of St John, showing details of the frescoed vaults (above, left), the amazing floors completely covered with tombstones (below) and the choir and high altar with the theatrical sculptural group of the Baptism of Christ (right).

The impressive Church of Our Lady of Mount Carmel with its unmistakable lofty dome.

THE CHURCHES OF VALLETTA

The Knights of Malta were, and still are, a religious Order so it should be no surprise that Valletta has a considerable number of churches. **Our Lady of Mount Carmel**, for example, was built in 1570 by Gerolamo Cassar but was rebuilt after devastating bombing in 1942. Completed in 1958 it now has an elliptical shape and, in particular, a soaring *dome* which dominates the city skyline with its 64 m. height. Just as outstanding is **St Paul's Anglican Cathedral** where the Gothic and neo-classical styles blend harmoniously. Commissioned and financed by Queen Adelaide of England (widow of William IV) who came to convalesce in Malta during the winter of 1838-1839, the Cathedral was designed by Richard Lankersheer to be built on the site of the **Auberge d'Allemand** which was demolished to make way for it, and was consecrated by the Bishop of Gibraltar. The organ came from Chester cathedral, but the most notable feature is the Gothic style *spire* which, at 166 metres, is visible from afar. The **Church of St Catherine**, used by the "Langue" of Italy, was designed by Gerolamo Cassar and in 1713 an elegant portico was added, the work of Romano Carapecchia.

Standing opposite the 16th-century church of St Catherine is the **Church of Our Lady of Victory**, another gem by Cassar, assisted on this occasion by Laparelli, and the first church to be built by the

Knights in Valletta in 1566 to celebrate victory over the Turks. On the instructions of Grand Master Perellos, the façade was renovated in 1690 with a bust of Pope Innocent XI. In keeping with the saint to whom it is dedicated, the **Church of St Francis** on Republic Street is simple and austere while the interior was elegantly frescoed in the 19th century with *Scenes from the Life of St Francis*. The **Church of St Paul's Shipwreck**, one of the largest in Valletta, was also planned by Cassar, though renovated first by Garagona and later by Gafà, and houses sacred relics of the saint who was shipwrecked on the island in 60 AD – a bone from his wrist and a fragment of the stone on which he was beheaded, a gift from Pope Pius VIII. The wooden statue of the Saint by Melchiorre Gafà kept in the church, is carried in solemn procession every 10 February, the anniversary of the shipwreck. Lastly, in the suburb of **Floriana** just outside Valletta to the south-west forming a sort of natural extension of the city towards the interior of the island, is the majestic **Church of St Publius** built in several stages during the 18th and 19th centuries to commemorate the first bishop of Malta. Damaged by bombing in 1942, it has two towers and an elaborately decorated interior. The famous *granaries* in the square in front of the church are quite impressive; these ancient underground deposits were capable of storing provisions adequate for two years and are closed by heavy circular stones seen in the pavement.

Left, Our Lady of Victory; below, St Francis.
Opposite: above left, the Church of St Paul's Shipwreck;
above right, St Catherine's; below, St Publius.

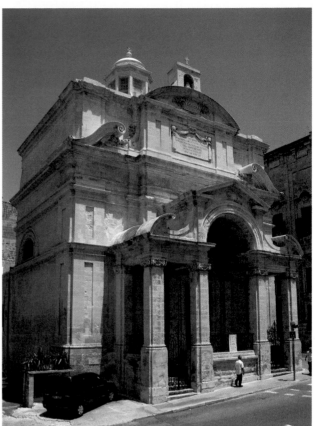

35

REPUBLIC SQUARE
NATIONAL LIBRARY,
ST JOHN'S SQUARE

Situated on Republic Street, *Republic Square* is also known by the older name of *Queen's Square* as it was originally named after Queen Victoria in 1897. An elegant *statue* of the queen, made by the Sicilian sculptor Giuseppe Valenti, dominates the centre of the square.

Overlooking it, with a façade of elegant arches, is the **National Library of Malta**, designed by Stefano Ittar, an architect from Calabria, and built between 1786 and 1796. Delayed by the French invasion, however, it was not opened until 1812. Today the library has some 61,000 volumes, 50 incunabula, 1250 illuminated manuscripts, the registers of the university from 1350 to 1818 and the precious archives of the Order (6,524 volumes dating from the 11th century on) which alone, as was evident as early as the mid 16th century, required the establishment of a public institution capable of archiving and conserving such important material.

St John's Square is also situated close to Republic Street, in front of the majestic Co-Cathedral of St John. With its elegant porticos the square is also a delightful area of pleasant cafés and open-air bars.

Republic Square, with its typical cafés and tables outside, is still also popularly known as Queen's Square after the regal statue of Queen Victoria (facing page, above).

Facing page, below, a view of busy St John's Square.

The **Cordina Café** is steeped in history. This fascinating locale in the heart of Valletta on Republic Street is no longer only an elegant café but also has a small restaurant that produces delicious masterpieces of Maltese cookery: from *Timpana* (baked maccheroni) to *Pastizzi* (savoury mille feuilles with ricotta cheese, peas etc.) and *Quassata* (a pie of ricotta, spinach, olives and anchovies). The building where it is located is also historic (the ancient "House of the General Treasury" at the time of the Knights, then public offices and subsequently the Grand Hotel and Malta's Casino). The origins of the business are historic, as the first Cordina Café dates from 1837 and the traditions and principles on which it was founded - elegance, products of excellent quality in a highly refined setting - were confirmed by Cesare Cordina who opened the shop in Valletta in 1944, and are still maintained today. The amazing decoration of the interior is entirely in harmony with these founding concepts. The ceilings are delightfully frescoed by the Maltese painter, Giuseppe Cali who has illustrated symbolically the various roles played by the island of Malta throughout the centuries. The Cordina family only recently commissioned the last two works portraying the independence of Malta and the birth of the Republic.

THE GRAND MASTERS' PALACE

Valletta is a city of palaces but for the Maltese, the Grand Masters' Palace is known simply as *il Palazz*, the Palace. The first building there was a plain wooden structure surrounded by a stone wall. The Order acquired it in 1571 but in 1572 the construction of the palace was still in its initial phase. Started by Grand Master Pietro del Monte, it fell to his successor, Jean Levesque de la Cassière, to complete the building. Subsequent Grand Masters, whose home it was, added their improvements and embellishments; the covered wooden balconies were added as late as the middle of the 18th century.

In its finished form the Palace is built on two floors and occupies an entire block. The two main portals, baroque and imposing, stand in direct contrast to the unadorned treatment of the rest of the façade; three other side entrances give on to as many streets. The Palace has all the hallmarks of its Maltese architect, Gerolamo Cassar: outwardly austere and sombre but extremely dignified.

Three of the doorways lead to a spacious courtyard while another portal and a gate lead to a smaller courtyard on a slightly higher level. Each of the two courtyards has a fountain against the wall opposite the main entrances; both are ornamental but, in their time, their function was more utilitarian than for mere show. On the walls of the *cloister* surrounding Neptune's Court-

The simple but sombre façade of the Grand Master's Palace, where the typical wooden balconies extend for some 89 metres (above). Opposite page, one of the splendid coats of arms that decorate the marble floors of the corridors on the first floor; below, the statue of the god Neptune dominating the courtyard named after it, and a view of the complex clock with four dials which can be seen in the smaller courtyard.

yard are sculptures of coats of arms that were removed from bastions and public buildings by order of Napoleon, some of which were defaced at the same time.

As in Renaissance palaces in Italy, the most important floor was the first, the **Piano Nobile**, the ground floor being used as stables, service quarters and stores. The **Main Staircase** leading up to the Piano Nobile was built by Grand Master Hughes de Loubenx Verdala identified by the wolf in the coat of arms. This staircase has been built to the same plan as that of Verdala Palace, the imposing country retreat of the same Grand Master. Both staircases have the same shallow steps, allegedly to make it easier for knights in heavy armour to climb them. The top of the staircase gives on to a lobby formed by the angle where two of the palace corridors meet. The right-hand passage leads to what used to be the Palace **Armoury** but that part of the building is now the seat of the House of Representatives (the Parliamentary Assembly is composed of only one chamber, there is no Upper House). Arrangements are in hand, however, to move the House into the Auberge de Castille. The *lunettes* over the windows in this passage are the work of Nicolò Nasoni da Siena and were painted in the first quarter of the 18th century. The corresponding works were painted by the Maltese artist Giovanni Bonello some 166 years later; together, however, the two series are complementary and show Maltese and Gozitan landscapes as they appeared at those times. The walls are hung with full-length portraits of various Grand Masters, one of whom, Jean Paul Lascaris Castellar, has entered the Maltese language: when a Maltese wants to describe a morose person he will say that he, or she, has Lascaris' face! The **Council**, or **Tapestry**, **Chamber** in the Armoury Corridor is an impressive hall where the

The larger of the two courtyards is known as the **Neptune Courtyard** after the bronze statue of the god there. This figure was placed in its present position by the British Governor, Sir John Gaspard le Marchand who had had it removed from another part of Valletta; the face bears a striking resemblance to that of Grand Master Alof de Wignacourt who originally commissioned it.

The smaller courtyard - the **Prince Alfred Courtyard** - is named after one of Queen Victoria's sons to commemorate his visit to Malta in 1858, but it is better known as that of **Pinto's Clock**. This clock has four dials showing - besides the time - the day, the month and the phases of the moon. The hours are struck by bronze effigies of Moorish slaves wielding sledge-hammers. It is said to be the work of the Maltese clockmaker Gaetano Vella and was made in 1745.

members of the Order sat in Council. On being elected to office, a Grand Master was expected to make a gift to the Order - the Gioja. Part of the Gioja of Grand Master Ramon Perellos y Rocaful was the price-less set of **Gobelins Tapestries** that give the name to this chamber. Perellos was elected in 1697 but it was only in 1710 that these tapestries were completed and hung in the place for which they had been created. *Les Tentures des Indes* (the Indian Tapestries) is a rather vague title for the magnificent rendering of fauna and flora from three continents, the Noble Savage also being very much in evidence. The space between the top of the tapestry to the ceiling is taken up with scenes depicting naval battles and other activities of the Order's galleys; the different panels are divided by twelve allegorical figures representing as many Christian and Ancient Roman virtues.

Pride of place is a picture of a *Crucifix* to remind the Knights that they were, first and foremost, a religious order. At the time the Tapestry Chamber was being used as the House of Representatives, during one of the more heated debates, a Member threw an inkpot at the head of his opponent; unfortunately the ink-pot missed its mark and hit the tapes-try instead. The ink stains have been removed but after this episode MPs were only permitted the use of pencils inside the Tapestry Chamber. On one side of the door to the Tapestry Chamber is a sort of niche protected by a grill; this niche is really the top of a well, a shaft in the thickness of the wall being connect-ed to an ancient cistern. Tradition has it that once a year, water was drawn from this well in a silver bucket and a goblet of the water was presented to a member

of the Sciberras family, Maltese aristocrats, by the Grand Master in person. The presentation took place inside the Tapestry Chamber as a symbolic payment by the Order as compensation to the previous owners of the land on which the Palace is built.

The first door to the right of the lobby leads into the **State Dining Room**. Here the British connection is well represented by several royal portraits: King George IV, who was Prince Regent when Britain took Malta under its wing in 1814, is portrayed, as is also Her Majesty, Queen Elizabeth II who was also Queen of Malta until the Declaration of the Republic of Malta in 1974. She is still held in high honour by the Maltese people as Head of the Commonwealth to which the island belongs.

The next door along the Entrance Corridor leads to the **Hall of the Supreme Council**, also known as the **Throne Room**. Like all the other ceilings of the Piano Nobile, the wooden ceiling of this hall is elaborately coffered and painted, but the item of greatest interest here is a *frieze of twelve frescoes* by Matteo Perez d'Aleccio who worked in Malta between 1576 and 1581.

These frescoes depict the most important events of the Great Siege and are particularly interesting as they were executed some fifteen years after that siege, and therefore well within living memory of those who had taken part in it. In the panel showing the *Arrival of the Piccolo Soccorso* (the Little Relief), the troops are being ferried across to Birgu and, among the rowers is a brawny Maltese woman, symbolic, perhaps, of the entire Maltese population that played such an active part in that epic siege. Against the far end of the wall is the **throne**, occupied first by the Grand Masters and then by the British Governors. Above the throne now are the arms of the Republic of Malta. Across the hall and opposite the throne a carved

Minstrels' Gallery is set into the wall; this carved and painted gallery is said to have been part of the Order's flagship, the Great Carrack of Rhodes, one of the vessels that carried the Knights to Malta. Yet another name for the Throne Room is that of the **Hall of St Michael and St George** - the two warrior saints who gave their name to an order instituted by King George IV in 1818. Investiture of members to that order was held in this hall, hence its name.

A door from the Throne Room leads to the **Ambassadors' Room**, also known as the **Red Room** from the colour of its damask hanging. The painted frieze shows the *History of the Order before its arrival in Malta* and deals mostly with the history of the Order during its long sojourn in Rhodes. In one of the panels, Knights of the Order are shown holding shields bearing the white eight-pointed (or Maltese) cross on a red background; this could be poetic licence on the part of the painter because the battle standard of the Order was a plain white cross on a red background, not unlike the Danish Flag; the white eight-pointed cross on a black background was more in the nature of a badge of the Order. On the walls of the Ambassadors' Room, rather appropriately, hang the portraits of a number of foreign

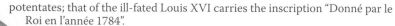

potentates; that of the ill-fated Louis XVI carries the inscription "Donné par le Roi en l'année 1784".

A door from the Ambassadors' Room leads to the **Paggeria**, the Pages' Waiting Room, also known as the **Yellow Room** after the gold damask covering of its walls. Originally the Grand Master had eight pages, but this was later increased to sixteen. The painting of the *frieze* is again by Matteo Perez d'Aleccio and the subject matter is a number of *Episodes in the history of the Order in the Holy Land*; the eight panels are divided by the inevitable allegorical figures, the one symbolising Republican Government being a strange intruder in the realm of those autocratic rulers - the Grand Masters of the Order. A door from the Pages' Waiting Room leads into a corridor which is at a right angle to the Entrance Corridor. This is known as the **Prince of Wales Corridor** in commemoration of a visit by King Edward VII, then Prince of Wales, in 1862. As a continuation of those in the adjoining corridor, the *lunettes* in the Prince of Wales' Corridor are likewise adorned with the achievements of the Order's galleys. These scenes recall the naval exploits of the Knights and

Inevitably the extensive picture gallery of the Grand Master's Palace in Valletta has numerous official portraits of the Grand Masters who lead the Order over the centuries, including Martin de Redin (above left) and Nicola Cottoner (below right).

add a decorative touch to the Grand Masters' Palace; but to the student of Naval History they are a mine of information since each picture carries a caption giving the date and describes the action depicted in the lunette.

The rooms along this passage were formerly the **private apartment of the Grand Master**; later they were used as the offices of the British Governors. These rooms are now the offices of the President of the Republic.

The British Governor, Sir John Gaspard le Marchand (1858-64) paved the corridors of the Piano Nobile with marble and embellished the floor with coats of arms. Originally the *sitting room* of the Grand Master, one of the rooms in this wing is decorated with a frieze of frescoes illustrating the birth of the Order. On the walls of this room are portraits of various Popes: as a religious order, the Knights acknowledged the Pontiff as their supreme head and it was to the Popes that the Knights turned as the final arbiter of their internal disputes. The *private chapel* of the Grand Master was turned into an office for the use of the Governor's Secretary and the minstrels' gallery, now in the Throne Room, was originally here. The paintings in this chapel are probably the earliest found in the palace and show *Episodes from the life of St John the Baptist*, the patron saint of the Order. The ground floor of the palace is now occupied by various government offices, including a number of Ministries and what were previously the palace stables now house the Palace **Armoury**. The armoury was transferred to this part of the palace when the original Armoury was transformed to house the House of Representatives. The original Palace Armoury served both as a Trophy Room and as an arsenal. Since all arms and armour of the Knights of the Order, other than their swords and daggers, became the property of the Order at their death, the Armoury was always well-stocked. The finer suits of armour were carefully preserved while the less important pieces were kept in the Armoury to be used as necessary.

Obsolescent arms were replaced with more modern ones from time to time; this applied particularly to firearms. The Knights frowned upon the use of firearms as being unchivalrous but they were obliged to move with the times. Registers of the arms were scrupulously kept and any removed had to be accounted for and, at times, a refundable deposit was collected from the persons to whom they had been issued.

Unfortunately the contents of the Armoury were less well protected in subsequent periods and innumerable pieces have disappeared, some to reappear in the Louvre and in the Tower of London. Fortunately some fine specimens have been preserved, particularly the *suits of armour* of some of the Grand Masters.

As presently displayed, the collection of the **Armoury Museum** is small but interesting; in the old Armoury, and even more so in engravings of the Armoury as it once was, one is impressed by the great number of exhibits, but on the other hand, many of the specimens were repetitious and to the serious student a specimen collection is more interesting. At the time of the arrival of the Order in Malta, in 1530, the use of firearms was rapidly revolutionizing warfare - the Great Siege was fought largely with artillery and arquebuses but armour still had its uses - a century later breastplates and shields were still being tested against firearms, and in the Armoury there are several examples with dents in them to prove that they were "bulletproof". Another exhibit that combines the old and the new is a *sword* incorporating a wheel-lock pistol.

FORT ST ELMO

Where in the 15th century a watch-tower stood, in 1551 the first fortress was built, and fifteen years later it managed to resist relentless bombardment by the Turks for an entire month. When it was finally taken all the occupants were massacred but by then it had become legendary. As a result Francesco Laparelli, an architect, was immediately commissioned to improve the defensive structures and the fort took on its present appearance, despite mainly superficial alterations and extensions carried out between the 17th and 18th centuries. Currently, the Fort houses the island's **Police Academy** and the National **War Museum** where items relating to the Second World War are displayed including the only biplane to have survived the war.

On Guard
One of the most fascinating events at Fort St Elmo, this historic pageant in costume with a military parade is set at the time of the Knights.
Alarm!
Another historic pageant, dating on this occasion from the period of French occupation, takes place every third Sunday of the month, also at Fort St Elmo.

Images that emphasise the solidity of the massive structure of Fort St Elmo showing also the original star-shaped plan; the National War Museum is now housed here.

dent Roosevelt around the island of Malta. Here too is the famous St George's Cross presented by the king of England to the people of Malta for the courage they had shown. The gallery of photographs illustrating the sacrifices that the local population suffered is also extremely interesting.

National War Museum

The National War Museum was opened in part of Fort St Elmo in 1975. Thus displayed in the old munitions deposit are some interesting exhibits from the time of the Second World War such as weapons and planes, and the jeep nicknamed "Husky" that escorted General Eisenhower and Presi-

45

In 1592 the Jesuits established the original "Collegium Melitense" for the teaching of philosophy, theology, grammar and humanities, with the addition, prompted by the advent of the plague, of the teaching of medicine in 1675. This has developed into the modern **University of Malta** which opened its new *campus* in the early 1970s in Msida, a suburb of Valletta.

Many events have troubled the history of the university over the centuries: with the expulsion of the Jesuits from the island it was transformed into a public university and was later peremptorily closed during the period of Napoleonic domination. Alexander Ball was responsible for reinstating it and restoring its ancient and prestigious role, while the English established the university statutes drawing on the example of British institutions. Today the University of Malta is widely renowned and also has an excellent library.

Msida

On the coast to the north west of Valletta a pretty village has developed around *Msida Creek*, a deep inlet part of which was filled in after the Second World War using the rubble and debris of ruins strewn throughout the capital following severe bombing. Once a busy fishing port, as the name of the village recalls (*msida* means "fishermen's refuge"), this is now a renowned **tourist port** which is always filled with boats. There is a lovely view of Valletta from here.

Sliema

The name of this town is derived from the Arab meaning "Greetings!" and recalls the traditional salute of the Maltese sailors to the church of Our Lady as they entered or left the port. The church stands near to Fort Tigne and was in fact destroyed in 1798 by Maltese cannon fire when the islanders revolted against the French. The town is situated on the jagged peninsula which forms the north-west side of the port of Marsamxett. With almost 40,000 inhabitants, Sliema is the most populous and active centre of the entire archipelago. But it has developed really only quite recently as in 1833 it was still considered "a small residential village for the citizens of Valletta in the summertime". According to the census of 1861 Sliema had only 324 inhabitants in addition to the wealthy Maltese who had chosen this spot, facing the sea and with an unencumbered view, as their holiday resort. Ever since then Sliema has grown and become known mainly for the excellent facilities offered by this pleasant tourist destination where, in addition to the tourist industry, business and crafts activities also thrive.

The elegant and majestic parish church of Msida dominates the busy tourist port. Facing page, views of Sliema.

St. Julian's

North of Sliema, this old fishing village developed around the Chapel of St Julian in an area where many of the Knights' hunting lodges were situated. Today this is a busy tourist area and seaside resort, even more peaceful, elegant and better equipped than Sliema. St Julian's overlooks a delightful narrow bay and the coast road along this beautiful part of the shore is quite lovely. In the mid 16th century it was in this bay that the fearsome pirate, Dragut Rais, landed with his large and legendary fleet, with the intention of supporting Sulieman the Magnificent in the conflict against the Order of the Knights. The plan was in vain however, as Dragut Rais met his death in St Julian's.

Boats

Malta is an island, the realm of fishermen, with a history of seafaring. It is no surprise therefore that one of the island's best known symbols are the highly coloured boats which are derived from ancient Phoenician vessels. The *Luzzu* is the traditional fishing boat while the *Dghajsa* is not unlike the Venetian gondola, but more colourful, and was used for transporting people and goods. The *Dghajsa* is now only seen in the Grand Harbour. On the prow of these boats is the unmistakable *Eye of Osiris*, Phoenician in origin and a symbol of protection for seafarers.

A typical scene of St Julian's where old and modern buildings surround the edge of the bay.

The typical little narrow streets of the town wind up along the rise of the coast to reach the impressive **Spinola Palace** dominating the bay from on high and surrounded by magnificent gardens. The original building dated from 1688 and was the pleasant summer residence of Paolo Raffaello Spinola from Genoa, the bailiff (or administrator) of the Order. Its present appearance dates from the 18th century renovation carried out by Spinola's grandson and designed by the architect Carapecchia. During the First World War the building was used as a military hospital.

St Julian's has many attractions including the *Casino* and the rough and **rocky coast** where, despite everything, unusual structures that are quite comfortable have been created, intended to make bathing easier and to enable visitors to sunbathe and relax. And here too, at the far end of the bay, is a genuine rarity for Malta – a tiny *beach* of fine golden and compact sand, a little corner of paradise resting in the sun and representing a spot much frequented by tourists, although its tiny size means that access to has to be restricted.

More views of St Julian's, a renowned sea resort and prestigious tourist destination; modern in its appearance, the town extends around the deep bay which is continuously patrolled by fleets of boats.

Paceville

Entirely devoted to entertainment, Paceville is quite a compact area not far from St Julian's and extremely well-known. It is no exaggeration to say that the most interesting night life of Malta takes place here in an amazing concentration of restaurants, pubs, discos and fashionable bars that are crowded all night long with bright multi-coloured lights illuminating the dark, while music of all kinds fills the air. Paceville really comes to life after dusk sets in and most of the clubs do not close until after 4am and some even remain open until dawn. There are many famous clubs, from the Portovino to the Fuego and the Bamboo Bar offering a vast range of choice – from Latin America to tropical – in sophisticated locales that cater for all tastes. Discotheques too provide an amazing variety of the latest music. And for those who are more romantic, what could be nicer than enjoying a drink on the beach under the stars.

Paceville is a modern centre not far from the coast and beaches of St George's Bay, and is particularly well known for its extremely lively and exciting night life.

Portomaso Tower

A spectacular group of attractive modern and even futuristic constructions can be seen in the area of St Julian's forming a dramatic and intriguing architectural development created out of the rocky coast. Portomaso is a diversified complex of buildings that, in 2000, was awarded a prize as the best "Marina Development" in Europe. While its function is primarily touristic and residential, it also comprises offices and various services. The complex extends along the side of a natural inlet which had to be modified to accommodate the requirements of the project, and now quays and wharfs have transformed it into a busy and well-equipped tourist port. Thus, facing right onto the sea, there are now prestigious hotels, including the famous and elegant Hilton, extensive residences and apartment buildings and, in particular, a lofty tower, the Portomaso Tower which has become the highly visible symbol of this resort. One hundred metres high, with 22 floors, the Tower houses numerous offices and on the lower levels there is also a conference centre. At the base of the south east side is a low curved stone structure supported by columns which link the tower and the conference centre, both also served by underground car parks, shops and more offices while all around the area roads built with a gradual gradient form a network specifically planned to facilitate traffic flow. The entire complex has been planned to provide the most futuristic and innovative architectural and technological features, remaining however, in harmony with the unique natural context.

*Images of St Julian's, showing the Casino (opposite).
The town is located on a rocky coast which is well-equipped
for the comfort of bathers.*

Maltese nights: it all happens in Paceville!

The true centre of Malta's nightlife, Paceville's discotheques can boast a clientele that is both numerous and international. Many young people come to frequent the bars and clubs which are capable of satisfying all kinds of musical preferences and interests. Maltese nights echo with the beat and rhythms of the most diverse types of music, from hip hop to reggae and soul. But live music is not neglected and there are frequent performances of both rock and blues bands. Memorable nights of entertainment under the starry sky of the island of Malta.

Gzira and Manoel Island

Not far from Valletta, Gzira is a peaceful and elegant residential town with a busy seafront and port that is always crowded with boats. A bridge crosses a narrow canal, some 40 m. wide linking the town to Manoel Island, a small island dividing Marsamxett Harbour into Sliema Creek and Lazzaretto Creek. Situated on this island is **Fort Manoel**, one of the best-preserved fortresses in Malta despite damage caused by bombing during the Second World War. The Fort was built in between 1723 and 1732 to house a garrison of 500 men, by the Grand Master Manoel de Vilhena who thus gave his name not only to the Fort but to the island where it was built; previously the property of the Chapter of the Cathedral of Mdina, the land had been known as the Bishop's Island. Also on the island today are the remains of the *old St Roch isolation hospital* and a modern shipbuilders' yard for yachts.

Għargħur

A typical little village resting between the sea and the bare hills of the north coast, Għargħur is noted for its *old cottages* built between the 18th and 19th centuries and still perfectly preserved and highly characteristic. The *Parish Church of St Bartholomew* is an impressive 17th-century building on which Tommaso Dingli worked, among others. The portal is quite splendid and the interior is decorated with interesting paintings dated 17th and 18th centuries.

Għargħur, resting between the sea and the slopes of the hills, has an elegant parish church.

57

Generally called the "Three Cities", the towns extending towards Valletta, dividing the Grand Harbour into deep inlets, are known historically with different names but those most commonly used today are **Vittoriosa**, **Senglea** and **Cospicua**. Originally a small settlement, Birgu (now Vittoriosa), developed here followed by a small fishing village around an ancient castle on the furthest point of a peninsula. This castle, known as Castrum Maris or Castell'a Mare, is mentioned in many medieval documents. When the Knights arrived in 1530, they decoded to establish themselves in Birgu as Mdina, although larger, was considered too far inland and they immediately began work on the fortifications of the village. Shortly afterwards the neighbouring peninsula, previously uninhabited and known as "L'Isla", was also fortified with ramparts and began to thrive, eventually becoming known as Senglea City in honour of Claude de Sengle who was, at the time, Grand Master. During the siege of 1565, the inhabitants of Senglea and Birgu showed such courage that the two cities received the honorary titles of "The Victorious" and "Invicta" (indomitable) respectively. The agglomeration that subsequently developed between Senglea and Birgu became known as Bormla and as successive Grand Masters continued the task of enclosing the Three Cities within an impressive circle of fortifications, Bormla became known as the "Cospicua" (the Notable City).

When Valletta was built, the Knights moved their government there form Birgu, but the Three Cities continued to be the centre for the Order's naval operations. Shipyards and arsenals were located there and Maltese sailors and ships' suppliers lived here. Under the British the cities were a real hive of activity as the Grand Harbour became the base of the British fleet in the Mediterranean. Due to this strategic importance, over time the cities have suffered from bombings and attacks which have not, however, affected the atmosphere of this urban complex which can still fascinate and charm the visitor.

of the naval shipyards continued uninterrupted, bringing wealth and prosperity to the town, but also heavy bombing during the Second World War. Today, however, a detailed and thorough programme of restoration has returned to town to its original, historic splendour.

Vittoriosa

Of the Three Cities, Vittoriosa is without doubt not only the oldest and most easterly, but historically is also the most important. The first port of the island in chronological terms, it developed around an earlier Fort St Angelo and the settlement, its defences further reinforced, was originally known as *Birgu*, a corruption of the Maltese word for "borough".

When, shortly after arriving on the island, the Knights of Malta chose Birgu as their first capital, the town flourished rapidly and soon palaces and *auberges* were built as well as churches and a new harbour and marine structures. Even when, after the great Siege, the Knights felt the need of a new, more suitable capital and transferred the centre of their operations to the new town of Valletta, Vittoriosa continued to remain for many years a bishopric and headquarters of the Inquisitor. In the centuries that followed, the development and expansion

Views of Vittoriosa, showing the elegant outline of St Lawrence's Church.

MARITIME MUSEUM

Opened in 1992 in what was once the bakery of the British Navy, the Maritime Museum of Malta describes the island's complex seafaring history. Numerous models of ships and boats are exhibited here together with paintings and ancient instruments.

NATIONAL MUSEUM OF ETHNOGRAPHY

The Museum is housed in the *Inquisitor's Palace* in Vittoriosa and this 17th-century building is, in effect, an outstanding home for this unusual museum. The *Hall of Justice* and the *Tower* where prisoners were kept are certainly fascinating, though the private apartments are also extremely interesting. Displayed in one of the rooms are some unusual instruments relating to the Inquisition as well as some religious artefacts.

FORT ST ANGELO AND FORT RICASOLI

Two old and mighty fortresses still survive as evidence of Vittoriosa's strategic position; as well as Fort St Angelo, already described, nearby on the parallel peninsula further west, extending across Grand Harbour, is the 17th-century Fort Ricasoli, almost a twin structure that still retains its original impressive appearance.

From top, the Maritime Museum, the National Ethnographic Museum located in the Inquisitor's Palace, and the impressive structure of the Żabbar Gate.

With its unusual scenery, **Malta and its archipelago have become an ideal film set** and thus a popular location for some quite famous films. The islands have in fact provided the memorable setting for such famous films as "Troy" with Brad Pitt in the role of Achilles, and "The Gladiator" with Russell Crowe, both real mythological blockbusters, as well as "Pinocchio" and "The Count of Montecristo", not to mention television series and numerous beguiling adverts. The *Rinella Movie Park* near Kalkara has actively welcomed and promoted this role, becoming an excellent model of how to happily combine the various requirements of tourism, history (with the nearby Cottonera fortifications) and entertainment facilities. The large salt water pools here provided a perfect set for filming scenes such as those in "Orca" and an episode in the series "Jaws".

Above, right and below right, views of Fort St Angelo; below left, Rinella Movie Park.

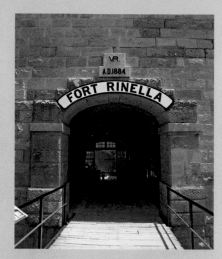

Fort Rinella is interesting from many points of view, but especially historically as this is one of the few Maltese forts not to have been built by the Knights of St John. It is in fact a Victorian fortress now famous for the gigantic cannon, known as the **Armstrong Cannon** that is located here. Concerned by the complete technological refurbishment of the Italian Royal Navy's weaponry after the dramatic battle of Lissa, the British Royal Navy commissioned the cannon to be built identical to those of the Italians at the factory of Sir William George Armstrong; it has a 450 mm calibre, is more than 9 metres long, and weighs 103.64 tonnes. The enormous mouth is capable of firing shells weighing a tonne at a distance of eight miles. A pair of these incredibly powerful cannons were located on Malta in fact, but proved also to be incredibly expensive as far as maintenance and effectiveness were concerned; one was situated to the east of Grand Harbour, and the other to the west of the Marsamxett port. It took three months of hard work in the autumn of 1882 to position the cannon at Fort Rinella. However, these two enormous war machines saw little activity and earned little glory as they were rarely used and never in a war. Today only that of Fort Rinella remains (its twin was completely dismantled in the 1950s) and, with its counterpart on Gibraltar these are the only 100 tonne Armstrong cannons in the world.

The Cottonera and Margarita Lines

One of the Knights' greatest and most constant worries was how to defend of the strategic position of the Three Cities and render them impregnable. It is no surprise therefore that in the 17th century it was decided to protect them by building a double stone wall, formed by two lines of defence, one external (the Cottonera Lines) and the other internal (the Margarita Lines). The aim of the project was to enclose within these walls a large area of protected land, capable of supporting some 40,000 people with livestock and food supplies in the case of siege. Thus in 1638 work began on the Margarita lines, intended to enclose Cospicua and the nearby hill which was of great strategic importance. Six ramparts were planned of which three were built immediately and three later, between 1716 and 1736. The impending danger of the Turkish menace (the fall of Candia, valiantly defended by the Venetians, took place in 1669), encouraged Grand Master Nicola Cottoner to bring Maurizio Valperga, military engineer to the House of Savoy, to Malta to undertake construction of the Cottonera Lines, built between 1670 and 1680. These consisted of a semi-circle of almost 5 km in length, protected by eight ramparts and two half ramparts; in 1675 the elegant *Żabbar Gate* was opened in the walls, its form recalling a triumphal arch. These defensive works were not completed as the funds for their construction ran out, however they did reach a quite impressive stage of development which would have required the use of several thousand men to guarantee an adequate response to an eventual siege. In fact, the two gigantic fortifications were never to experience such a baptism of fire and now remain primarily as impressive evidence of the heights reached by military and defensive engineering on the little island of Malta, continually in the front line before the Turkish threat.

Between Kalkara Creek and Rinella Creek, sheltered by the peninsula where Fort Ricasoli stands (below left), is the little village of Kalkara, overlooked by the silvery dome of the elegant parish church.

Senglea

Enclosing the three deep inlets that were transformed into the dry docks of active naval shipyards in the past, this is the most western of the three peninsulas forming the south eastern section of Grand Harbour. For a long time it remained uninhabited until, that is, it was realized that Vittoriosa required the best possible protection. Thus first Fort St Michael was built at the end of the western peninsula. Between 1553 and 1557 a small village developed here, surrounded by parks and gardens and soon fortified by Grand Master Claude de la Sengle, for whom the town was then named. Having gloriously survived the Great Siege, Senglea continued to grow and prosper, developing into an attractive town. Centuries later, in 1922, the fort was completely dismantled. Some twenty years later, terrible bombing during air raids by the forces of the Axis attempted to destroy the great naval shipyards and continued for more than two years from 1941 to 1943. Senglea was destroyed and the entire population was

evacuated. Reconstruction, unfortunately not entirely harmonious or consistent, was carried out around the few large monuments that had survived and are still visible today, overlooking the dense network of narrow streets. The most outstanding of these, on *Triq il-Vitorja*, the main street of Senglea, is the **Church of St Filippo Neri**, also known as Our Lady of Porto Salvo, a 16th-century structure refurbished several times in the course of the 17th century. The church of **Our Lady of Victories**, designed and built in the 17th century by Cassar was seriously damaged during the war and has been tastefully reconstructed. The church houses many works of art, including the much venerated statue of

Maltese Dghajsa

One of the most typical boats to sail the seas of Malta are the *Dghajsa*, of Phoenician origin; brightly coloured, they are exactly like gondolas and have been used for centuries to transport goods, people and sailors who had to join their ships from the land. Production of these gondolas is very limited today and they are mainly used for the traditional naval competitions in which genuine historic events from the times of the Knights are represented.

the Redeemer (*Ir-Redentur*) and the statue of Our Lady, also known as the "La bambina", traditionally lead in procession on 8 September every year (the date of the birth of the Virgin) to solemnly commemorate the end of the Great Siege. Without any doubt one particularly pleasant feature of Senglea is the small but delightful **public garden** (*Safe Haven Gardens*), located on the ramparts from where there is a stupendous panorama of Valletta and the port. Situated in the gardens is a famous *lookout post*, a watchtower with relief sculptures in stone of a pelican, an ear and an eye, symbolising the Knights' constant watchfulness against their enemies, and the importance of the port to the Maltese.

One of the most famous attractions of Senglea is the unusual hexagonal watchtower with its unusual decoration, in the Safe Haven Gardens.

Cospicua

Protected by a massive stone wall and by the two peninsulas of Senglea and Vittoriosa that encircle its bay, the town first came into being as a small fishing village, for long known as *Bormla* until it was given its current impressive name by Grand Master Marcantonio Zondadari who, during the first half of the 18th century, decided to commemorate the courage shown by the inhabitants during the Great Siege of 1565 with this title.

For a long period the town's fortunes depended on the busy naval dockyards at the end of *Dockyard Creek* where originally galley boats were produced and later modern ships of heavy tonnage. It was precisely because of these shipyards that Cospicua became the target of heavy bombing during the Second World War. Today, with 10,000 inhabitants, Cospicua is a densely populated and flourishing town, one of the most important industrial centres on Malta, although the narrow medieval streets and the mighty defensive walls enclosing it might seem little suited to accommodate modern industrial development. Among its most important monuments are the baroque **Church of the Immaculate Conception** (16th-century but refurbished on several occasions) and the 17th-century **Church of St Teresa of Avila**.

Typical views of Cospicua: above, the entrance on the south, Port St Elena; left, one of the characteristic old stairways; right, a shining statue of the Virgin, much venerated in Cospicua and in the Three Cities in general.

The Megalithic Temples

Ggantija

This complex on the island of Gozo, consists of two temples side by side and is the oldest example of a megalithic temple in the archipelago, dating from a period between 3600 and 3000 BC. Built of flint and oxydian and enclosed within a ring of stone walls, they were probably used for propitiatory rites and reveal quite advanced building techniques (as seen, for example, in the remains of domes and the use of monoliths which would have been very difficult to transport). Recent excavations have brought to light a series of rather curious statues, with oddly tapering heads that are highly distinctive.

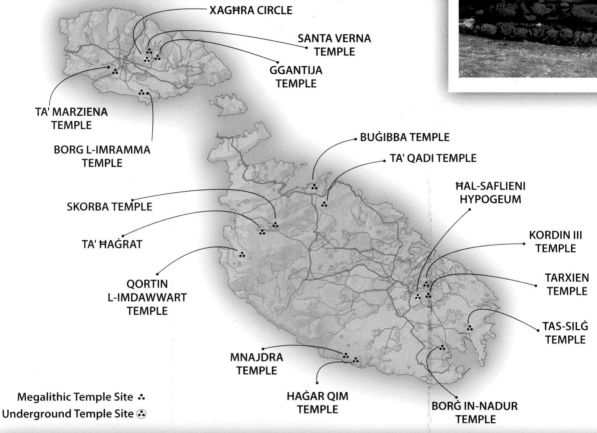

XAGĦRA CIRCLE

SANTA VERNA TEMPLE

GGANTIJA TEMPLE

TA' MARZIENA TEMPLE

BORG L-IMRAMMA TEMPLE

BUĠIBBA TEMPLE

TA' QADI TEMPLE

ĦAL-SAFLIENI HYPOGEUM

SKORBA TEMPLE

KORDIN III TEMPLE

TA' ĦAĠRAT

TARXIEN TEMPLE

QORTIN L-IMDAWWART TEMPLE

TAS-SILĠ TEMPLE

MNAJDRA TEMPLE

HAĠAR QIM TEMPLE

BORĠ IN-NADUR TEMPLE

Megalithic Temple Site ⁛
Underground Temple Site ☉

Tas-Silġ

Tas-Silġ is an ancient place of worship (dating from the 4th millennium BC) which continued to be used over a particularly long period. Detailed research, supported by archaeological excavations, has in fact confirmed that the temple continued to be used as such even at the height of the Iron Age. Moreover the Italian Archaeological Mission, which lead an important programme in Malta in the 1960s, succeeded in bringing to light in the area surrounding the temple not only the remains of interesting structures dating from the earliest period, but also evidence that the Phoenicians had reused the temple complex, probably during the first millennium BC. However, it is quite likely that the great temple of Tas-Silġ still has numerous fascinating secrets to reveal.

Ħal-Saflieni

Recently restored, this complex of temples is on three levels underground reaching a depth of 12 metres. Built in different stages from 3000 to 2000 BC, Ħal-Saflieni is noted for a spiral staircase that is surprizingly modern both in form and concept. Unique of its kind, in the early 20th century the temple risked irreparable damage from a building site created for the construction of a new complex. Sir T. Zammit, the foremost patron of Maltese archaeology, fought energetically and effectively to save the site which was then studied in depth between 1905 and 1911. Consequently it was discovered that the first and oldest level had been created from natural caves, while the two below, representing two different periods (the first contemporary to the Ggantija temple complex, and the second to Tarxien) are more sophisticated and elaborate achievements, with larger rooms and walls that are more competently finished and decorated. The most interesting rooms are on the second level, such as the *Oracle Room* and the *Holy of Holies*. The roof of the first is decorated with a warm red and is covered with original spiral motifs that flank and entwine with quite elaborate drawings of trees. The holy of holies is instead one of the most elaborate rooms, with stone walls that have been engraved and polished. From here there is access to the lower level where there are further rooms dedicated to ritual functions, and a well. This hypogeum was also used as an ossuary and the remains of about 7,000 skeletons were found here. It therefore seems probable that the temple ceremonies were related in some way to the cult of the dead. In any case it seems probable that the hypogeum was in use until 2000 BC.

Tarxien

In no other place on Malta are the buildings of prehistoric temples better documented than in the megalithic temples of Tarxien. The first temple, now in ruins, is the oldest, dating from about 2200 BC, while the more recent structure dates from some 400 years later. The *spiral* as a decorative motif appears in various parts of Europe, from the north Atlantic coasts to the Aegean; the Tarxien spiral is unusual in that it was invented independently. The most colossal *stone statue* of this period was discovered inside these temples; originally 2.5 metres in height and probably representing a Mother or fertility Goddess, the statue was divided into two parts and the upper section is now missing. Many theories exist concerning the meaning of the statues of the "fat women" found in almost all the Maltese temples, and they may be examples of female fertility deities. About 1800 BC, the temples, abandoned for about 200 years, were reused by peoples of the Bronze Age for cremation and to bury the ashes of their deceased.

Ħaġar Qim

This Copper Age temple was originally built about 2700 BC but even then it underwent several modifications.

For some unknown reason the axis of the first structure was altered and the temple itself was several times extended.

The kind of stone used in the building of this temple (Globigerina Limestone) is rather soft and relatively simple to work; possibly for this reason there are several "porthole" openings in Ħaġar Qim.

A *monolith* on the outside of the temple wall has been tentatively interpreted as evidence of phallic worship. A *pillar "altar"* with an unusual palm frond decorative carving has been found in this temple, but not in any other; it is possible that the pillar was not originally part of the temple furniture and was placed there at a later date.

Mnajdra

Perhaps having learned that Globigerina Limestone does not resist bad weather, the builders of Mnajdra constructed this temple out of the harder Coralline Limestone which, however, was difficult to work, while the interior walls were faced with a softer kind of limestone.

The best preserved of the three Mnajdra temples it is interesting for the secret chambers that are hidden inside the thickness of its walls; these chambers communicate with the temple itself by holes bored through the wall; it is surmised that statues of gods or goddesses could have been placed in front of these holes and the "priest" hiding in the oracle chamber was the voice of the deity as it "spoke" to the faithful. A healing cult may well have been practised in this temple as a number of baked-clay models of parts of the human body, showing symptoms of disease, have been found here.

Żabbar

Outside the Cottonera Lines, to the south east of the Three Cities, the town of Żabbar developed significantly from the 18th century on, around an existing and impressive parish church. At the end of the 18th century its strategic position was exploited by the English in their battle against the French troops, but also brought Żabbar under heavy bombing during the Second World War. Its principal monument is, however, still the **Church of Our Lady of Grace** commissioned by the parish priest, don Francesco Piscopo, begun in 1641 and completed, according to some, in 1660, according to others in 1696. A Maltese saying maintains that "A church is never finished" and in fact parishioners are never entirely happy with their own church and as far as they can, continually try to improve it as their village church must always be bigger and better than that of their neighbours. And the people of Żabbar were no exception: with the considerable funds provided by Andrea Buhagiar, the parish priest, and collected by the residents themselves, work to improve the church began in 1738. The Maltese architect, Giovanni Bonavia, redesigned the façade and added two bell towers while internally the church was given a marble floor and a crypt. The most important painting here is the *Madonna and Child* by Alessio Erardi (1669-1727).

Marsascala

This old fishermen's village, nestling at the end of the Marsascala bay, was sacked and devastated together with the surrounding area in 1614 when the ferocious Ottomans landed, taking advantage of the lack of any substantial de-

fence (there were only two small forts to discourage possible invasion, Fort St Thomas and Fort Zonqor). In the centuries that followed, Marsascala remained mainly a harbour and fishing port frequented by many fishermen, including Sicilians. During the 20th century, however, Marsascala discovered tourism and opened its wharves to yachts, adapting its infrastructures to the requirements of an ever increasing number of tourists, both local and foreign. Now, during the summer, this pleasant and well-equipped sea resort is one of the most popular on the island, yet it is still possible to see the age-old scene of fishermen mending their nets or attending to their unmistakable and colourful boats.

Birżebbugia

This small town, the name of which means "Village of the Olives", developed recently on the headland that extends between St George's Bay and Pretty Bay. It is noted for the 18th century *Pinto Battery*, created precisely to defend this headland, and now flanked by a monument commemorating the meeting between Gorbaciov and Bush which took place in 1989. Quite nearby is the *Ghar Dalam* cave where many extremely interesting fossils have come to light, the most ancient yet found on Malta.

Left, the Church of Our Lady of Grace in Żabbar; below, two views of Marsascala and its magnificent coast; right, a view of Birżebbugia.

Għar Dalam

A real natural gem, the cave of Għar Dalam is on the coast not far from Birżebbugia, below the unusual St George's Chapel. In the era when the Maltese islands were an extension of the Italian mainland, animals like elephants, hippos, deer and foxes roamed the land. With the rising of the sea-level, or the sinking of the land, or both, the islands were separated from the land mass and these animals were marooned. This took place in the Quaternary Era, some 10,000 years ago, and not during the Pliocene, eleven million to one million years ago, as was once thought to have been the case.

In time these stranded animals gradually evolved into an island sub-race resulting in a degeneration in some of the species.

Fossil bones of animals have been discovered in caves and fissures in various parts of the island, but the largest concentration to be discovered so far is that at Għar Dalam. In 1917 two human molars were found in this cave and, at the time of their discovery were believed to be those of Neanderthal Man.

However, these molars have now been assigned to a much later period and it can be assumed that when the animals died, and their bones were carried into Għar Dalam by the action of flowing water, man had not yet arrived in Malta. Stone Age man did use Għar Dalam as his abode around 4000 BC but, by this time these animals had become extinct in the Maltese Islands.

Marsaxlokk

Marsaxlokk, the harbour to the south-east, is now a small but picturesque harbour where the brightly coloured fishing boats ride at anchor and where the wives of the fishermen knot nylon string bags for the tourists. But Marsaxlokk is also a microcosm of the historical past of the Island. A short distance from this village is the archaeological site of *Tas-Silġ* still in the process of being excavated; the remains of Late Neolithic megalithic buildings have been found here, greatly modified by superimposed Punic and Byzantine structures; here too are the only remains of a mosque to be found on the island. Norman coins have also been found at Tas-Silġ.

Views of Marsaxlokk: right, the 19th-century Church of Our Lady of Pompeii, almost on the shores of the sea, and the characteristic boats; below, Fort St Lucian.

To prevent the landing of corsairs in the harbour, the *Fort St Lucian* was erected at its entrance by the Order. Used as a munitions depot during World War II, it now houses the Marine Research Centre. Marsaxlokk Bay, of which the fishing harbour of Marsaxlokk forms part, is now being converted into a port for container ships.

The Sunday market

The port of Marsaxlokk is strongly identified with its traditional activities and is also famous for the crowded market which takes place here every Sunday. As might be expected, this is principally a fish market, held right on the seafront but close also to a general market where there are many stalls displaying numerous varieties and types of lace.

Marsaxlokk is widely known for its traditional boats "with eyes", the **luzzu**; it is traditionally believed that these eyes (of ancient Phoenician origin) protect the boats from danger.

Wied iż-Żurrieq and the Blue Grotto

The western coast of Malta is steep and precipitous but in places clefts in the cliffs slope down to sea-level. One such cleft is Wied iż-Żurrieq. Looking like a miniature fjord, this narrow arm of sea

Enchanting views of Wied iż-Żurrieq (above left) and surroundings, with the coast and the Blue Grotto (top).

provides anchorage for boats in calm weather; at the first sign of a storm the boats are winched up a steep slipway and landed. The boats at Wied iż-Żurrieq were, and still are, used for fishing; now, however, the fishermen are discovering that it is more lucrative to take visitors to the nearby **Blue Grotto**.

The presence of this deep sea-cave, in which the sea depths are of an unbelievably intense blue, has long been known to the fisher folk. During World War II, when an air-raid alarm was sounded the inhabitants took to their boats and rowed into the cave for safety.

The island of Filfla

With its unmistakable outline, rocky and inaccessible, some 700 m. long, Filfla rises out of the sea 5 km. south west of the island of Malta. Mainly sheer and arid, somewhat inhospitable at first sight, since 1988 this fascinating little island has been recognised as a nature reserve: in fact, unique to the island and highly adapted to the conditions is an endemic species of green lizard with red markings (*Lacerta muralis* var. *filfolensis*). Only one small chapel, dated 1343, has been built on the island over the centuries though it was destroyed by the earthquake of 1856. For several decades after this its only rather curious role was to provide a target for bombardment in war training for the ships of the Royal Navy and by the Royal Air Force.
The most famous of the legends told about this island relates that in the distant past God wished to punish the inhabitants of il-Maqluba for their dreadful wickedness, and so plunged them into hell with all the land that surrounded them. But so vicious were they that even the devil did not want them and he decided to throw them back up to the earth with all their land, thus creating the inaccessible and deserted shred of land that rises out of the sea and is known by the name of Filfla.

Dingli

Standing at a height of 250 metres, this village offers a magnificent panorama: the sea, the small island of Filfla and the Buskett Gardens are all visible from here. Not far from this little village are the **Dingli Cliffs**, which look truly impressive especially when seen from the sea. A small *chapel*, built in honour of Mary Magdalene stands here and also indicates the highest point of the island. The slopes of the hillsides are terraced for agricultural production.

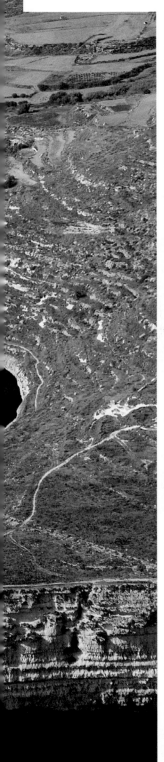

Verdala Palace and Buskett Gardens

The Verdala Palace in Buskett is now used by the president of the Republic for representation purposes and heads of state on official visit are housed here. Designed in 1586 by Gerolamo Cassar (who also designed St John's Co-Cathedral), it was built for the Grand Master and cardinal Hughes de Loubenx Verdala as a country villa surrounded by beautiful gardens. The countryside all around was called *Buskett*, from the Italian word "boschetto" meaning woods. The villa is constructed on a base surrounded by a moat which is crossed by a flight of stairs. These lead to the ground floor where there is a spacious stairway, famous for its vault decorated with frescoes portraying the achievements of the Grand Master. A lovely elliptical stair leads to the first floor. A *chapel*, dedicated to St Anthony Abbot, where a painting by Preti is housed, is found in the Buskett Gardens where cypresses, oaks, pines and ashes thrive as well as orange and lemon trees, the fruits of which are gathered and sold during the Christmas period. A competition of ballad-singers, known as the *ghanja*, is held in the garden every year.

Siġġiewi

A pretty and peaceful village that has always lived from farming, Siġġiewi was one of the first ten parishes created on the island in 1436. Narrow streets and lanes lead into the large central square where the grand **Church of St Nicholas** stands. Built between 1675 and 1693 and designed by Lorenzo Gafà, this splendid building is one of the finest and most opulent examples of baroque architecture in the archipelago, revealing an Italian influence in general, and Sicilian in particular. The extraordinarily elaborate façade and the dome, however, were restructured and altered in 1864 by Nicola Zammit. The interior is richly decorated and the church houses an unfinished masterpiece representing *St Nicholas*, by Mattia Preti. Two other religious structures, the **Church of the Assumption** and the **Church of St John**, are also of interest.

The highly elaborate and splendidly decorated Church of St Nicholas overlooks the main square of Siġġiewi, while its dome is visible from everywhere in the village.

Rabat

Both Rabat and Mdina are perched on a ridge overlooking the whole expanse of the island and the sea beyond. Both centres have been inhabited for thousands of years.

Rabat incorporates much of the old Roman city which was reduced to its present dimensions by the Arabs.

Consequently the sumptuous townhouse with its fine polychrome mosaic pavements, which was once inside the Roman town of Melita, is now actually part of Rabat and houses the Museum of Roman Antiquities.

In the Roman era the Melita area was enriched with palaces and temples, relics of which, such as inscriptions, columns, capitals and mosaics, are now in the Museum of Roman Antiquities.

The Rabat area is closely connected with the introduction of Christianity to the islands: in 60 AD St Paul the Apostle, under arrest on his way to Rome and shipwrecked on the island, is said to have lived for three months in a cave within the ditch below the walls of the old Roman city – St Paul's Grotto – which he used as a centre for his activity in establishing a primitive Christian community.

Since then the area has been dedicated to St Paul and is overlooked by a church where an important cemetery flourished in medieval times.

Burial being prohibited inside the walls of the city, the area outside the ditch, from St Paul's Grotto to Buskett, abounds with a concentration of hypogea - or burial places - of pagan, Jewish or Christian origin dug into the rock by the Phoenicians, Greeks, Romans and Byzantines. Their tombs contain a rich variety of architectural elements. The largest of these are the St Paul and the St Agatha complexes in the Hal-Bajjada district.

Before the Knights arrived, Rabat had become the centre for various religious orders which preferred to build their houses not far from the capital city but at the same time sufficiently secluded for their monastic retreat.

The Knights, concentrated in Vittoriosa and Valletta, erected very few buildings in Rabat and did little to embellish the area.

Today, besides schools and colleges, Rabat has various social clubs and musical bands, a market which is very popular on Sunday mornings, and sports fields. The Rabat area is ideal for walks in the countryside.

ST PAUL'S COLLEGIATE CHURCH

St Paul's Collegiate Church is constructed upon, but to the left of St Paul's Grotto, just outside the walls and in the ditch of the old city, hence reference to it as St Paul Outside The Walls in old documents. The earliest documentary evidence referring to it dates from 1372. A medieval cemetery with many private chapels and memorials flourished to the left of the church. The dedication to St Paul is due to the traditional belief that St Paul used the cave as a base for his preaching and to create a Christian community

Interior and exterior of the Collegiate Church of St Paul with, above right and below, three views of St Paul's Grotto, a catacomb where an expressive statue of the saint is located.

during his three months' stay in Malta in 60 AD. For this reason St Paul's Grotto was described by the Cathedral Chapter as "the foundation stone of the Church in Malta". Grand Master Alof de Wignacourt transformed the church into a Col-legiate of the Order, constructed a college for chaplains officiating the new institution and erected a College as well as a new church of St Publius, adjacent to St Paul's Parish Church. The Order of St. John enriched the building with various works of art, including a fine altarpiece with St Publius by Mattia Preti, an altarpiece of the *Eucharist* by Francesco Zahra (1710-1773), a *statue of St Paul* over the altar in the Grotto executed by the Maltese sculptor Melchiorre Gafà though completed by his master Ercole Ferrata, following Gafà's death and a fine 18th-cent. Neapolitan organ by Giuseppe del Piano. Among its works of art are three paintings by Stefano Erardi (1630-1716) and the huge altarpiece by Francesco Zahra of the *Holy Family* for a side altar. From Preti's workshop are *The Stoning of St Stephen* in the transept and *St Michael* as well as the oval depicting *God the Father* in the chapel on the right of the entrance.

This page and facing page below left, the Museum of Roman Antiquities showing some of the statues, mosaics and elegant rooms. Facing page, on the right, views of the St Agatha Catacombs.

MUSEUM OF ROMAN ANTIQUITIES

The misnamed "Roman Villa" Museum covers the site of a rich and sumptuously decorated town house that once belonged to a wealthy person in Roman Malta. The site, discovered in 1881 and further excavated in 1920-24, contains a number of remarkably fine **mosaic polychrome pavements** and some original architectural elements.

A number of rooms were constructed to protect the mosaics and an upper hall was added to provide exhibition space and a suitable entrance.

The porticoed neo-classical façade was completed in 1925.

The *mosaics* offer the main attraction, rated among the finest and oldest in the western Mediterranean they compare well with those of Sicily and Pompeii. Originally these mosaics paved the peristyle, once supported by 16 columns and two adjacent rooms. One of the pavements has only survived poorly in patches; the other rooms create an illusion of three dimensional depth.

ST AGATHA CATACOMBS

Not far from St Paul's Grotto, below the church of St Agatha, are spectacular catacombs dedicated to the saint and covering some 4,000 square metres, though only a very small area can be visited. The walls are decorated with numerous frescoes dating from the 12th to the 15th centuries, Byzantine in style and portraying scenes from the life of the Saint who is traditionally believed to have passed part of her exile on Malta. A small museum is situated beside the catacombs, displaying a wide range of antique objects including ceramics, clothing and coins.

STATUE OF A DRAPED FEMALE FIGURE, PROBABLY A PORTRAIT STATUE

1st Century AD
Domus Romana

Mdina

The Arabs divided the old Roman city of Melita into two: the citadel became known as Mdina (the city) and the rest of the area as Rabat (the suburb), names which are still used today. In medieval times Mdina was the seat of municipal government and an important administrative centre as well as the assembly point for military forces in case of enemy attack. During this period many religious orders built their monasteries outside the walls of Mdina, establishing themselves in Rabat and the vicinity. When the Order of the Knights arrived in 1530, they chose to settle near to the port where their ships were anchored, thus leaving Mdina and its inhabitants undisturbed. When Valletta was built and became capital of the Maltese islands in 1571

Mdina became known as the "Old City" and some of its residents moved to the new town. Among those who remained, however, were Malta's aristocratic families who continued to live in their ancestral homes with the happy result that a great number of 14th and 15th-century houses and palaces were preserved. The main entrance to the city was built in 1724 by Grand Master De Vilhena, replacing a drawbridge which is now walled up, though its outline can still be seen a few metres to the right of the existing gateway. A narrow stone bridge decorated with shields bearing arms sculpted in stone and flanked by lions crosses a moat which was excavated by the Arabs; the lion was part of the coat of arms of Grand Master De Vilhena. A Latin inscription on the exterior

Facing page, an aerial view of the city of Mdina which highlights the dense medieval urban structure and its original purpose as a fortified citadel.

Two of the most important entrances are the Main Entrance (above left) and the more austere Greek's Gate (left).

An unusual and very characteristic feature of Mdina are the numerous, elaborate door knockers, both old and more recent, which decorate the doors of palaces and houses in the town.

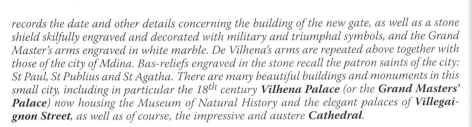

records the date and other details concerning the building of the new gate, as well as a stone shield skilfully engraved and decorated with military and triumphal symbols, and the Grand Master's arms engraved in white marble. De Vilhena's arms are repeated above together with those of the city of Mdina. Bas-reliefs engraved in the stone recall the patron saints of the city: St Paul, St Publius and St Agatha. There are many beautiful buildings and monuments in this small city, including in particular the 18th century **Vilhena Palace** (or the **Grand Masters' Palace**) now housing the Museum of Natural History and the elegant palaces of **Villegaignon Street**, as well as of course, the impressive and austere **Cathedral**.

THE CATHEDRAL

According to tradition, the first Cathedral of Malta was dedicated to the Blessed Virgin, Mother of God but, having fallen into ruin during the Muslim period, it was rebuilt following the Norman conquest and re-dedicated to St Paul. The old church was modified and enlarged several times; however, the dreadful earthquake of 11 January 1693 almost entirely

MDINA

destroyed the cathedral and only the sacristy and choir, which had both been recently built, were left standing. Construction of a larger building in baroque style began immediately and the Maltese architect Lorenzo Gafà was commissioned for the task. The new cathedral was completed and consecrated in 1702.

CATHEDRAL MUSEUM

On Archbishop's Square, the Cathedral Museum has been located in an impressive baroque palace, formerly a seminary, since 1969 and contains extensive artistic and archaeological collections as well as important archives. The most substantial part of the *artistic collections* comes from the legacy of Count Saverio Marchese (1757-1833). A large room is used for the temporary exhibition of new acquisitions, but is also available for local artists to exhibit their most recent work.

Right, the exterior of the Cathedral.
Below, Cathedral Museum, a tondo of the Umbrian School, portraying Saint Catherine, and the Expulsion from Eden *by Bernardo Strozzi.*
Opposite, view of a typical medieval street.

Ta' Qali Crafts Village

A military airport occupied this area on the road leading from Rabat to Mosta until the Second World War. But the air base had already been abandoned for some time when the empty hangars began to be used by a factory producing blown glass, and gradually the crafts village of Ta' Qali came into being. More crafts business began to occupy the other buildings and new structures were also added. Traditional items such as ceramics, gold and silver filigree and lace work were produced in the same location and other, sometimes less traditional, businesses also moved in. One of the new crafts that has developed here is the production of items in polished stone; Maltese marble is used as the raw material thus offering visitors the chance to take home a little piece of this wonderful island. A copy of armour (in various sizes), can be bought as a reminder of the history of Malta, or even a ceramic model of the famous Fat Goddess.

Mosta

Mosta is roughly in the geographical centre of the island of Malta, and in the past it was considered to be far enough inland to be relatively safe from pirate attacks. Given its position, Mosta is an important crossroads lying on the route for those travelling from the south and the east towards the north of the island.

The chief attraction is now the monumental church, dedicated to the Assumption and called **St Mary's**, with its circular design which was inspired by the Pantheon in Rome. Its *dome* is the third largest in Europe, the two other domes being in Rome and in London. The building was started in 1833 and the church was consecrated in 1871; it was built around and over an earlier church which continued to be used during

The dome's interior of the unmistakable round Church of St Mary in Mosta (facing page, above).

94

the period when work was in progress. In today's machine age it might seem that construction took an exceedingly long time, but it should be remembered that work on the church was done on a voluntary basis, in the little spare time that the labourers had at their disposal. Like many other of the old churches in Malta therefore, this is a true monument of faith.

In 1942 a thousand pound bomb penetrated St Mary's, piercing the dome and rolling through the interior but without exploding.

Today one of the main items of interest in the Church of St Mary is attributed to a great miracle worked through the divine intercession of the Virgin. Exhibited in the sacristy is the fearful bomb that, at 16.40 on 9 April 1942, crashed through the dome, bounced off the walls twice inside before coming to rest on the floor without exploding. Two others simply grazed the church and rolled into the square in front also without exploding. Hundreds of worshippers were attending Mass at the time, yet no one was injured.

St Paul's Bay

Located in one of the three largest, deepest and most famous bays of Malta, set between Qawra Point and the islands of St Paul, the town which was once a small fishing port is now (and has been for almost a century) a well-known tourist and seaside resort. Its history is linked to the life of St Paul who landed here in 60 AD following a shipwreck during his journey towards Rome. It was here that he quenched his thirst (and it is still possible to visit *Għajn Rażul*, the *Apostle's Fountain*); here it is believed the saint threw the snake into the fire (where today the *Church of tal-Ħuġġieġa* or church of the bonfire now stands); and here the Roman governor Publius welcomed him (the *Church of San Pawl Milqgħi* records this event and was

recently restored following severe damage by bombing during the last war). Yet the present and the future of this area are determined by the villas, the hotels, the modern tourist facilities, the restaurants, the clubs, marine centres - and therefore by an ever-increasing and regular tourism. Thus the large bay in the area to the south west (known as Xemxija) is a continuous series of residential zones linking St Paul's Bay to lively **Buġibba** and elegant **Qawra**.

The name of **Xemxija** is also known for a group of shaft tombs (dated between 2700 and 1600 BC) dug into the rocks and interconnected, that were discovered in 1955. On a hill not far away stands an 18th-century castle, or rather a palace built by Domenico Cachia and similar to the Verdala Palace; now an elegant hotel, **Selmun Palace** formerly belonged to the Mount of Redemption, an institution created to liberate Christians from Arab slavery.

Lying opposite this ring of peaceful bays, including pretty **Mistra Bay** which has long been famous for its tranquil sea and shelter from the winds, are the two **islands of St Paul** which are connected at low tide. On the first and largest of the two islands, named *Selmunett*, is a small chapel dedicated to the saint, and a white marble statue representing him that was made in 1845.

Views of splendid area of St Paul's Bay, with its rocky coast, inlets and the calm, crystal-clear sea: above, Buġibba, town waterfront with view towards Xemxija; right, from the top, Buġibba, Mistra Bay and the elegant Selmun Palace.

though excavations and restoration were not completed until 1953. The remains of the two buildings forming the site are rather limited but are in any case of great importance to better understanding the Maltese Neolithic period.

Nearby, the unusual *Zammitello Palace*, a curious and isolated 19th-century copy of the Tower of London is worth a visit.

Perched on high, dominating the bay which takes it name, Mellieħa is a typical village with houses built close around the unmistakable church, perfectly visible from afar.

Below, the church of Mġarr, dedicated to the Virgin Mary, Regina Coelorum.

Mellieħa

On old maps, two landmarks are indicated to the north of Malta: the salt marshes, and the old church of Mellieħa. The production of salt has been moved elsewhere (the old salt works were once sited where the *Għadira Bird Sanctuary* now stands), but the old partially **underground church dedicated to Our Lady** still stands here. According to tradition, a *fresco of the Virgin Mary* was painted by the apostle St. Luke who, with St. Paul, was shipwrecked near here in the year 60 AD. Scientific study of the icon has assigned it to a more recent, but still quite ancient, period.

Mġarr (Malta)

An isolated 19th-century village that developed in one of the most fertile areas with plentiful water, Mġarr, its name meaning "the market place", is an agricultural area specialized in wine-growing.

Two of its main attractions are the 20th century *church* dedicated to the Virgin, *Regina Coelorum*, clearly inspired by Mosta's circular church and, just outside the village, the *Neolithic temple of Ta' Ħaġrat* dating from about 2800 BC and rediscovered in 1925 by Themistocles Zammit al-

Għadira Nature Reserve

In the north west of Malta, situated between the two hills of Marfa and Mellieħa at the end of Mellieħa Bay and beyond the beach lies a marshy area of ponds where all the rain water that falls locally collects due to the morphological structure of the area. In the past the famous salt works were located here, though now they form a fantastic natural landscape where a well-known nature reserve, called Għadira (meaning "salt marshes"), has been located since the 1960s. Part of the marshes lie below sea level and consequently sea water also flows into the area forming salt water marshes, though the concentration of salt varies according to the amount of rain water that has fallen in any given period and to the height of the tides. An indication of this unusual feature can be seen in the vegetation that grows spontaneously around the pools of water consisting mainly of plants that are capable of surviving in salty environments. As a result this entire and somewhat unusual area rapidly developed into a safe and comfortable refuge for many endemic reptiles, insects (there are numerous butterflies) and small mammals. Of the many creatures that inhabit the pools some of the most fascinating are the gecko, the Mediterranean chameleon (a veritable attraction in Għadira with its fantastic ability to camouflage itself), the weasel, wild rabbits and bats. With the passing of time, however, and as a result of its particular environmental features, Għadira has increasingly become mainly a true sanctuary for the wild birds that gather here in great numbers in all seasons of the year. Ducks of all kinds, coots, moorhens, blue-tits, yellow wagtails and many other species too (from swallows to robins and kingfishers) – all are to be found here according to the time of year, including a considerable number of migratory birds. Given the increasing attention that the area began to enjoy on an international scale, it was officially recognised as a wild bird oasis in 1978 as a result of the interest and concern of the Malta Ornithological Society, which has continued its constant task of making the marshes as suitable and hospitable as possible (hunting and netting are absolutely forbidden) for birds, and animals in general as well, of course, as plant life. Thus the territory has been optimized and special small islands have been created, while a large number of trees are now planted around the perimeter of the reserve. In addition, particular attention has been devoted to education, intended to teach the tactics of observing bird life with the creation of a Visitors' Centre and promotion of numerous initiatives of interest to schools for which guided visits are available from Monday to Friday.

Red Tower

Glancing around Mellieħa Bay in the direction of the hills that rise behind it towards the interior of the island, it is not very difficult to imagine the strategic importance that this locality must have had in more belligerent and less scenic times. It is not therefore surprising that in 1565 as the Great Siege was coming to an end, history records the landing in this bay of some 8,000 men under the command of the viceroy of Sicily, prepared for a final and decisive clash with what remained of the Turkish troops, by then in retreat. It is not by chance then, that on the slopes of the hills leading north west to Marfa from Mellieħa Bay, the Red Tower – one of the seven watch towers built by Grand Master Lascaris – still stands, protecting the bay below. From here there is also an amazing panorama towards the north west and thus to the neighbouring islands of Gozo and Comino (providing an excellent field of vision, therefore) and towards the channel that separates them from Malta. Square in plan, this large and complex tower, reinforced and protected at the corners with four small keeps, was built between 1647 and 1649 and appears like an austere fortress the entrance of which was for long protected by a drawbridge. In 1649 the tower was supplied with heavy artillery and it is said that it was painted red (leading to the name of Red Tower, used instead of its official name of Fort St Agatha) in order to be more visible to the other guard posts in the surrounding area. It has recently undergone complete restoration.

Enchanting bays of Malta to visit:

The entire north and south-west coast of the island of Malta is formed by an uninterrupted series of bays, some deep, some broad and peaceful, creating a magnificent and fascinating landscape. Swept by the waves of a crystal sea, looking even more impressive with the wild rocky slopes that rise just behind the coastline, bear and rugged in appearance, these inlets are isolated and beautiful with an air of natural severity that makes them seem almost timeless. Yet it is not difficult to reach them as they are served by convenient roads and efficient bus routes and not far away occasional, yet large, tourist structures have developed.

To the north west, for example, just in front of the island of Gozo is the peaceful little **Paradise Bay**. Nearby **Anchor Bay** is pretty and unspoiled and its clear waters with an abundance of fish have made it particularly popular with skin divers, though it also was made famous by the film director, Robert Altman who had an unusual village built here for the set of his film, "Popeye". Continuing south along the coast is **Golden Bay** with its blue green sea and fine, firm and golden sand, as well as **Għajn Tuffieħa Bay**; both can be reached on foot by long flights of steps and are well connected to Valletta by bus and to St Paul's Bay by a convenient road that crosses one of the most fertile and luxuriant parts of the island. Yet further south is **Ġnejna Bay**, surrounded by imposing rock faces but with a splendid beach almost 300 metres long, and providing a peaceful refuge for those who wish to enjoy the sea and sun surrounded by the silence of nature. High above the *Lippia Tower*, an 17th-century watch tower built by Grand Master Lascaris, seems to be watching over the safety of the bathers.

Paradise Bay • Anchor Bay • Golden Bay
Għajn Tuffieħa Bay • Ġnejna Bay

One of the most intriguing amusement parks on the island of Malta is **Sweethaven**, the almost fairytale village of Popeye, created in Anchor Bay in 1979 as the set of the film made by Robert Altman recounting the adventures of the brawny sailor and his inseparable Olive Oil. Altogether 17 highly original little houses were made by teams of labourers with wood brought from Canada and the Netherlands for the purpose. When shooting of the film came to an end they were converted into an amusement park that is truly unique. Here children enter the magical world of Popeye where they can participate in shows and games, travel on a miniature train, experience the thrill of a mini-rollercoaster – and be photographed with the characters of this most famous cartoon strip.

GOZO

Some years ago it was planned to connect the islands of Malta and Gozo by a bridge and Japanese engineers were called in to carry out a feasibility study. The project was considered technically possible but as the expense involved would have been considerable the plan was shelved. And many people in Malta, and many more in Gozo breathed a sigh of relief.

It was feared that, should the island of Gozo become too accessible, there would be a real danger of the island losing the old-

world charm which Gozo has so far retained, and which Malta too once possessed but began to loose during the mid 20th century. Malta's smaller sister island is different in that it is more fertile and more picturesque, but what makes Gozo so markedly different from Malta are the Gozitans.

These frugal and tough people seem resistant to any adversity; their character is steel-like, tempered by privations and constant danger and, as a result of their frequent ordeals, they and their

descendants have emerged strong and resilient.

Malta and Gozo share the same history and similar historical remains are found on both islands, but Gozo has had more than its share of misfortunes. Largely undefended, the island has many times been devastated by pirate attacks and on one occasion almost the whole of the population was carried into slavery.

When Gozitans had advance warning of an impending invasion, such as the Great Siege, some of them sought refuge in the better fortified towns of Malta while the elderly were evacuated to Sicily, but they always returned home as soon as it was safe for them to do so. Gozitans ransomed from slavery also returned home, never thinking of nor wishing to settle in a safer place. Even Gozitan emigrants who become wealthy in the countries of their adoption likewise return home and build grand houses for themselves as evidence of their success. Perhaps what makes Gozo special is the love and quiet pride of its inhabitants for their homeland and this pride is reflected, among other things, in the size and beauty of their churches.

The love that Gozitans have for their homeland is contagious too. Many visitors have been fascinated by the island and have decided to remain, becoming Gozitans themselves (except for Ulysses who, after staying for seven years, renounced the charms of the nymph Calypso, who, it is said, lived on Gozo). Rural and romantic, perhaps – but not uncultured: opera singers of international fame are often invited to perform in the capital of Gozo, Victoria (Rabat was renamed in honour of Queen Victoria). Younger generations enjoy concerts by pop singers and the music festivals. Moreover, some of Malta's best brains come from Gozo. As in other rural communities, especially where economic conditions are hard, the Gozitans are parsimonious, but their frugality never sinks to the level of stinginess and their generosity in supporting worthwhile initiatives is unlimited.

Mġarr (Gozo)

The port of Mġarr is the foremost point of access to Gozo, where the ferries from Malta dock. And indeed the word *mġarr* can mean equally "market place" or "departure point". The neo-gothic **Church of Our Lady of Lourdes** was built in 1888 high on the hill that overlooks the main port and the more recent tourist marina and appears to welcome the boats as they arrive. On the left, at the top of the unmistakable blue-grey cliffs and also seeming to protect the quays and wharfs below, is the impressive *Fort Chambray* which was planned during the 1600s but only built in 1749 by the governor of Gozo, Jacques de Chambray. It was therefore the last fortification made by the Knights and valiantly succeeded in blocking invasion by the French after strong resistance to their advance in 1798.

Views of Mġarr, the island of Gozo's main port, overlooked by the elegant form of the Church of Our Lady of Lourdes.

beaches of Calypso's island

The small but delightful island of Gozo is noted for the beauty of its many little known and generally unspoilt corners as well as for its singular geological features. Amidst the impressive cliffs and natural pools of salt water there are magnificent inlets such as the splendid **Dwejra Bay** to the west with its amazing crystal clear water (following pages, showing the natural arch nearby known as the "Blue Window"), and **Xlendi Bay**, one of the few where the recent success of tourism can be seen (right). But there are also genuine small fjords, often etched out over the centuries by the sea, or that have developed along the fault lines of Malta (called the *wied*), such as the inviting **Mġarr ix-Xini** (below) and the **Ta' Ċenċ Cliffs** (left).

Fungus Rock

This cliff, over 50 metres high, is named *"Gebla tal-General"* (the General's Rock) by the locals as it is said that a Commander of the Order of St John discovered a *shrub* here which is known locally as *"Gherq Sinjur"* (*Cynomorium coccineum* Linn.). The plant was jealously protected by the Knights of St John as it was believed to possess great medicinal properties against certain ailments and illnesses. In 1744 Grand Master Pinto rendered the rock completely inaccessible. Until the middle of the last century the Government employed a guardian for Fungus Rock.

One of Gozo's many attractions, in addition to the cliffs formed by the sea and the winds and the stupendous isolated beaches (centre above, the red beach of **Ramla Bay**, the most famous of the island), are the characteristic *salt marshes*, basins of salt water usually linked to the sea by long tunnels (above left), and **Calypso's Grotto** of legendary fame (right, large photo). According to tradition, Gozo is identified as the island of Ogygia, where the nymph Calypso kept Ulysses for seven years, promising him immortality if he were to stay with her forever. Zeus intervened however, forbidding this destiny and Ulysses departed. Although it is difficult to compare the current state of the grotto and its surroundings with Homer's description of Calypso's residence in the *Odyssey*, prehistoric terracotta remains dating from the Ggantija period (c. 3600 BC), have been found just a few metres from the cave entrance.

Victoria (Rabat)

The Gozitans always use the name of *Rabat*; it is the only town in Gozo and was named Victoria in 1897 on the occasion of the Diamond Jubilee of Queen Victoria.

It is in the centre of the island and has been the capital of Gozo probably from Roman times. The Romans built defensive walls around the town which the Arabs continued to reinforce after conquering the island in 870 AD.

Nothing structurally very old has survived but in the haphazard, twisting lanes and alley-ways of the town, splendid balconies and grand palaces revealing features of local architecture are still to be seen.

The main Government offices are scattered in the centre of the town, while the banks, the main police station, the bishop's curia and the government secretariat for Gozo are in Republic Street.

Visitors will find a wide range of items in the many small shops, markets, boutiques and jewellery shops throughout Victoria.

THE CITADEL

The original nucleus of Victoria, the Citadel, is built on one of the many flat-topped hills in the centre of Gozo. Its origins can be traced to the late Middle Ages. At one time the entire population of the island took shelter within these walls at sunset. The walls themselves date from the 16th to the 18th centuries. Most of the buildings inside the Citadel are in ruins but the **Old Courts of Law** and the **Old Governor's Palace** are still being used as the Law Courts of Gozo. The **Old Prisons** and the **Armoury of the Knights**, the **Archaeological**, **Natural History** and **Folklore Museums** can all be visited. The **Cathedral**, together with the **Bishop's Palace** and the **Cathedral Museum**, dominates the Citadel.

THE CATHEDRAL

The Cathedral designed by the Maltese architect Lorenzo Gafà in the form of a Latin cross was built between 1697 and 1711 on the site of an older church. Inside, one's attention is drawn instantly to the trompe l'oeil *ceiling* depicting the interior of a dome painted by Antonio Manuele of Messina in 1739. Paintings by the Maltese artists Giuseppe Hyzler, Michele Busuttil and Tommaso Madiona are also found here. Equally interesting are the *high altar* inlaid with precious malachite and, on either side of the main door, the pair of *baptismal fonts* sculpted from blocks of Gozo onyx.

The ancient Citadel, with its imposing fortified enclosure, overlooks not only the city of Victoria, of which it forms the original nucleus, but also the entire island of Gozo. In the south east is the Cathedral dedicated to the Virgin Mary; above, the elegant interior.

Cathedral Museum

This building is at the back of the Cathedral.
The exhibits consist of *ecclesiastical vestments*, *decorations* and *paintings* – including a beautiful 15th-century panel painting – and the old *bishop's landau*. There are also numerous *portraits of bishops and dignitaries* providing a glimpse of some of the characters in Malta's history over the last few centuries.

Left, an internal view of the Cathedral.
Below, the Parish Church of St George.

Above, the Museum of Folklore where an old millstone is exhibited.
Right, some of the items housed in the Archaeological Museum.

FOLKLORE MUSEUM

This Museum is located in three late medieval houses with Sicilian-influenced architectural features.

Exhibits include *agricultural implements*, an old *millstone for grinding corn*, items related to the *cotton industry*, *tools used in the production of various crafts* and some *traditional costumes*.

ARCHAEOLOGICAL MUSEUM

All archaeological material found in Gozo is now exhibited in this 17th-century house known as the 'Casa Bondi'. Of special interest are some terracotta shards of the Ghar Dalam phase (5000 BC) found at Ghajn Abdul, probably the oldest ever found in the Maltese islands, and the *Majmuna tombstone*, a beautiful marble inscription in Kufic characters dating to 1174 AD.

It-Tokk

It-Tokk was the centre of Roman Victoria and was probably the market place, as it still is today. Archaeological excavations carried out in the square in 1960 revealed there had been human activity here as early as the Bronze Age (1500 BC). Interesting archaeological finds and structures show that the area was intensely occupied during the Roman period.

More items from the Archaeological Museum, including, above, the famous Majmuna tombstone.

In the morning It-Tokk is bristling with activity; a market is held where clothes and fabrics are the main wares for sale. In the side streets round the square one can buy the delicious Gozo nougat, the *"bankuncini"* (sweets made with almonds) and the *"pasti tassalib"* which are Gozo's sweet specialities.

Ta' Pinu Sanctuary

This is a national shrine and a centre of pilgrimage for both the Gozitans and the Maltese. On this spot there was a 16th-century chapel dedicated to Our Lady of the Assumption with an altarpiece painted by Amedeo Perugino in 1619. On 22 June 1883, Carmela Grima a middle aged peasant woman is reported to have heard the voice of Our Lady speak on this same spot and this was followed by numerous acts of grace and miracles of healing while Gozo also succeeded in avoiding the plague the following year. Offerings were sent to the chapel from all of the Maltese Islands, as well as from abroad. The present **church** was begun in 1920 and was consecrated in 1931. It was raised to the status of basilica by Pope Pius XI a year later. The old chapel with the original painting can still be seen at the very end of the church where votive offerings are hung on either side of the shrine. Built in the Romanesque style, this church rises isolated in the unspoilt Gozitan countryside surrounded by the hills of Għammar and Gordan. It is a perfect example of workmanship and craftsmanship in Maltese stone. Many intricate and varied designs are sculpted inside in the same stone, while mosaics adorn the altarpieces and the friezes of the aisle.

Xagħra

An ancient village in the centre of the north eastern plateau of the island, Xagħra has always been an agricultural centre and has a most elegant **parish church**; nearby are the famous **Ggantija temples**.

Above, the Ta' Pinu Sanctuary. Left and below, views of Xagħra showing its large parish church. Right, the church of St John the Baptist in Xewkija.

Xewkija

The **church** of Xewkija is dedicated to St John the Baptist and its dome is one of the largest in the world. The building was started in 1952 and finished in 1973. It was built round the previous parish church which continued to be used for religious functions until it was demolished in 1972. The dome of Xewkija was intended to be larger than that of the church of Mosta in Malta and in fact Xewkija is higher, but the diameter is smaller.

Besides an *altar panel* by Giacchino Loretta, a pupil of Mattia Preti, there are three excellent *works* by Francesco Zahra, the most important Maltese painter of the 18th century.

Attached to the Rotunda is the church **Museum**, where one can see the collection of the church *treasury* and some of the *sculptural works* from the old church which was a masterpiece of baroque architecture.

The numerous windmills of the Maltese islands were introduced by the Knights and are most useful for irrigating the fields. One of the most famous is the 18th-century **Ta' Kola windmill** which stands not far from Xaghra and the prehistoric temples. It has been converted into a museum.

Ggantija Temples

The Ggantija or, as it was commonly known in the past, "The Giants' Tower", is the largest, the best preserved and by far the most impressive prehistoric temple. It is probably the finest of all the ancient remains in these islands and can compare with Stonehenge for grandeur. It was uncovered about 1826.

Ggantija consists of two separate systems of courtyards which, as with the Mnajdra temples, do not interconnect. They are known as the **South Temple** which is bigger, earlier (c. 3600 BC) and better preserved, incorporating five large apses, and the **North Temple** which is smaller and a later addition (c. 3000 BC) with a 4-apse structure. The great court of the South Temple measures some 23 metres from one apse to the other, and the height of the walls here reaches eight metres, the highest of all the temples. The arch was not yet known at the time of their building and the span of the apses here is quite large

for any conceivable stone roofing. Wood or animal hides might originally have been used as roofing material.

Two kinds of stone were used in the construction; *"talfranka"*, the soft stone mainly used inside as portals and floor slabs, and *"talqawwi"*, a harder stone which is mostly used for the general construction of the walls. The interior was plastered and painted with red ochre. The huge megaliths forming the outer wall (the largest weighing several tons) were built alternately, one horizontally and one upright.

The space between the inner and outer walls is filled with rubble and earth and it is this system which has given the Ggantija the necessary stability to withstand the depredations of more than 5,000 years.

The floor is partly covered with soft stone slabs and partly with turf, or beaten earth. Spiral and pitted designs decorate some of the soft stone slabs.

The impressive remains of the two great megalithic temples of Ggantija; although they are fundamentally massive ruins, amazingly it is still possible to imagine their primitive magnificence despite being extremely ancient.

The lace of Sannat

Without any doubt, Sannat is the historic home of the famous white and cream coloured laces made on cushions by the expert and speedy hands of the women of the village. This tradition has been passed down over the centuries from generation to generation, and was highly appreciated even by Queen Victoria.

Gozo has a variety of high-quality crafts production. A visit to the **Ta' Dbiegi crafts village** is extremely interesting and it is also possible to watch items being made with blown glass.

Sannat

Sannat is the most southerly village of the island. The **church**, dedicated to St Margaret, was built in 1718 to replace a smaller one after Sannat had become a parish in 1688. The main *altar panel* was made by Stefano Erardi. Another important work is the *St Francis altar panel* by Francesco Zahra. Near to the church is an old lime kiln, no longer in use. Going to the left of the church, at the top of the hill, **Ta' Ċenċ** is famous for its cliffs.

San Lawrenz

Leaving the village of Ta' Dbiegi, before turning towards the left and the internal sea, is the **Church of St Lawrence** with *paintings* by Giuseppe Calì, Attilio Palombi and Gianni Vella. The writer Nicholas Monsarrat lived and worked in this village for many years until his death in 1979.

Żebbuġ

Like most of the churches on Gozo, the **Church of the Assumption** in Żebbuġ, the most northerly town on the island, is an impressive baroque structure. Consecrated in 1726, it was the first church to be built with aisles on Gozo. Various sculptural works in local onyx, such as the *high altar*, enhance the interior.

Marsalforn

This is the best known holiday resort on Gozo and the harbour is always busy, especially in summertime. Originally a fishing port, the colourful boats can still be seen in a sheltered corner of the bay and fresh fish is available in the restaurants all year round. All kinds of marine sports can be enjoyed here and, in addition, Marsalforn has an attractive sandy beach with hotels, bed and breakfast, apartments and shops that are well stocked with souvenirs.

Above, two views of the Church of the Assumption in Żebbuġ with a detail of the cannon that still looks as if it is protecting the entrance. Below, a view of Marsalforn, a renowned and well equipped seaside resort on the northern coast of the island. Opposite page above, the Church of St Margaret in Sannat; below, St Lawrence's.

COMINO

COMINO AND COMINOTTO

COMINO AND COMINOTTO

For long periods of its history Comino was an unsafe place in which to live, nevertheless, people did inhabit this tiny island lying between Malta and Gozo at various times, and the population fluctuated from zero to just a few inhabitants.
In 1416 the Maltese petitioned the Aragonese king, Alphonse V, to build a tower on Comino as a deterrent to the corsairs who made it their base, but the people of the island had to wait two hundred years before work began and the Tower of Comino was only finally finished under Grand Master Alof de Wignacourt in 1618. Despite the protection of the tower, people were wary of making Comino their home and the ancient church here was, in fact, deconsecrated in 1667 as it was derelict; in 1716 it was repaired and re-consecrated and by this time the island had been repopulated to some extent.
With its handful of resident families and a single hotel, even now the atmosphere and landscape on Comino is that of a deserted but very beautiful island.

COMINO AND COMINOTTO

COMINOTTO

Uninhabited and bare, the little island of Cominotto is immediately to the west of nearby Comino; the two islands form a small channel, named the **Blue Lagoon** for its amazingly blue and crystalline waters. In 1993 much of the channel was closed to shipping to make it pleasant and relaxing for bathing.

St Mary Tower

St Mary's Tower is a sturdy watch tower, built by Grand Master Alof de Wignacourt in 1618, that still dominates the south western part of Comino.

With its splendid islands and the blue unspoilt sea, the islands of the Maltese archipelago are now recognised as a real paradise where enthusiasts of skin diving can fully enjoy their favourite sport. Clear transparent waters, rocky sea beds and fascinating inlets provide spectacular diving, both in the caves and in the open sea both for those who are expert and for learners. The clear seas are also perfect for those who wish to try some underwater photography. Many surprising sights are to be discovered amidst the labyrinths formed by the caves, little channels and cliffs that look like delicately embroidered rocks – as well as luxuriant and colourful plant life, and magnificently brilliant fish that venture close to the coast, there are also fascinating wrecks that still remind us of the distant yet dramatic events of war.

Index